The Sacred Bond

---

7 SPIRITUAL TRUTHS
TO RECOGNIZE AND MARRY
YOUR VERY OWN SOUL MATE

DR. GRACE CORNISH

MCDONALD-LIVINGSTONE
NEW YORK

Published by McDonald-Livingstone
Web: www.mcdonaldlivingstone.com
E-mail: livingstonebooks@aol.com
Phone: 212-576-8811

Editorial: Public Relations:

610 Fifth Ave   786 Bronx River Road
P.O. Box 4739   Suite #B-33
New York, NY 10185   Bronxville, NY 10708

ISBN 0-9630654-5-9
Library of Congress Control Number: 2004118431

Cover design by Sharon Lewis
Front cover photo by David Beyda
Back cover photo of author and husband by Tyrone Rasheed
Interior book design and typesetting by Melecia Livingstone

This is dedicated to you...

> **Two are better than one because they have a good reward for their labor...if two lie together, then they have heat, but how can one be warm alone?**
> (Ecclesiastes 4:9 & 11)

It's simply your turn to be loved.

Acknowledgments

A special heartfelt thanks to these fantastic individuals who directly and specifically influenced the completion of this book project:

♡Richard, my sacred soul mate husband
♡Dena, my sacred little princess
♡ Helen, my awesome editor
♡Sharon, my dynamic cover designer

Sincere appreciation to my friends, fans, and associates who continue to support and encourage my work – and also to *you*, for allowing me to minister to your mind, heart, and sprit (Enjoy!).

Contents

Introduction

> ## "Whatever is truly yours, can never be taken away from you!"

It never ceases to amaze me how God works! I believe that God has created a sacred soul mate for each and every individual. But too often we choose incorrectly and prematurely, and therefore either end up in mis-matched unions or remain being lonely and yearning for compatible love throughout our individual life span on Earth. All of this is about to change.

In your hands, you are holding a Holy Spirit-filled, practical and effective relationship guidebook that will show you how to recognize and marry your very own soul match. Forget the outdated myth and falsehood that you can't find real love when you are purposely looking for it. Yes, you can. I certainly did, and so have thousands of other women, just like you. The key is to know where to look, how to look, and what to look for. These are God's promises to you and me, "If you seek, you will find, if you ask, it will be given to you, and when you knock, it will be open to you."

Unlike fictional fairly tales, I don't believe in Cinderella's match-making fairy godmother, but I do believe and have proven that a real life God-the-Father has created and set up the soul-mate, sacred match system from the beginning of time. This is accurately recorded in the book of Genesis where the Lord said, "It is not good for man to be alone. Therefore shall a man leave his father and his mother, and shall cleave [bond] unto his wife, and they shall be one flesh." This bond is a sacred bond.

You are entitled to have your very own sacred, happy, healthy, love relationship and marriage with your very own soul mate. Whether it's your second, seventh, or seventeenth time looking for the right relationship, it doesn't matter. What matters is this manual will equip you with the information to get it right this time around. Marriage is a good thing. A good marriage is fun and it enriches your life. It's wonderful to experience the joy and companionship of compatible love. Sacred love is a healthy, rewarding balance between the two people involved, with no third party interference. It's a universal truth that "if something is truly yours, it can never be taken away from you." This means you can relax and be your true self. You don't ever again have to live in fear of losing out on true love. When it is meant to happen, it certainly will – at the right time.

I believe your time has come and it's now your turn to experience sacred love. If it weren't, you wouldn't be holding this book. I don't believe life is based on luck or coincidences. I believe in blessings, proper planning, and purpose. It is truly no coincidence that you happened to pick up this book, or that someone gave it to you. Whether you're single, divorced, widowed, in a common-law arrangement, or are a woman who has everything she desires – except the right husband – these time-tested spiritual truths will surely lead you to the altar, to be wedded in holy matrimony side-by-side with your special soul match, who cherishes, adores, and loves you, just for who you are.

The Sacred Bond is designed for women of all ages, at various stages in their lives. You don't have to be physically perfect by anyone's standard to attract your perfect match, but you need to be spiritually and psychologically healthy to attract a mate who is equally yoked. This book is a companion guide to *The Band-Aid Bond: How to uncover the hidden causes and break the patterns of unhealthy loving.* I have received numerous e-mails, letters, and phone calls from some of the thousands of women throughout the country and around the globe who've already benefitted from the relationship restoration program in that guidebook. Through word-of-mouth publicity, these women have helped *The Band-Aid*

Bond to become a national and European bestseller which continues to help thousands to *resolve* the causes of unhealthy love, *dissolve* their past emotional pain, and become prepared to *evolve* to a higher level of living through sacred loving.

I've purposely included the term "recognize" in the subtitle of *The Sacred Bond: 7 spiritual truths to recognize and marry your very own soul mate*. That's because while you're reading this book in preparation to meet and marry "the one," God can be simultaneously putting the man who will be your ideal life partner through his own growth stage in preparation to meet you at the right appointed time. Isn't that awesome? Want to hear something even deeper? It is very possible that you've already met your soul mate and hadn't "recognized" him at the time because either you weren't ready for the healthy love you were entitled to, or you could have been caught up in a counterfeit relationship with the wrong man, or maybe you were recovering from the hurt of a past relationship. Think about this as you read through this book.

I wouldn't tell you this if it was not true. It happened to me. I shared the story of my relationship at the end of *The Band-Aid Bond*, and I will introduce you to the importance of "spiritual recognition" here and elaborate further along in the book. I met Richard (my handsome, chocolate sacred soul mate hunk of a husband), two years before I realized that he would be the man I'd be spending the rest of my life with. He knew it at first sight, because he was already prepared through his own personal relationship with the Creator. I was still a work in progress.

I felt an inner pull towards him, but I paid no attention to it because I had my head buried into my career and wasn't ready for a relationship at the time. We lost contact shortly after our initial meeting. When I was ready to meet and marry my own soul mate, I took the matter to the Creator of all souls. Since I believed that He made me, I was sure that He had also made the ideal match for me. I was ready for the *real thing*, so I contacted the *right One* – I contacted *God*.

I prayed, believed, and I received three proposals within a one-year period. I relied on my God-given intuition and discerning spirit to guide me and I chose wisely. I chose Richard (and he chose me simultaneously). I humbly, honestly and happily share with you that I am experiencing a sacred love and healthy bonding greater than I ever imagined.

This is my exact wish for *you* also. God has promised that "Where two or three are gathered together in my name, I am in the midst of them; and anything you ask in my name, *believing*, you shall have it." I live and govern my own life by this truth and I openly share it with you here. Throughout this book, I will be standing in agreement with you, *believing* that God will connect you with the healthy, sacred bond that you desire and deserve to have.

For this cause a man shall leave father and mother and cleave [bond] to his wife and the twain shall be one flesh...What therefore God had joined [connected] together, let not man put asunder.
(St. Matthew 15: 5 & 6)

Spiritual Truth # 1:
"You Are Wonderfully Made"

KNOW YOUR SELF-WORTH

You are in for a fantastic treat! This specially-prepared guidebook will show you how to recognize and marry your very own soul mate in a manner that is spiritually-sound, psychologically-healthy, emotionally-fulfilling, and physically-nurturing.

Isn't this awesome? I'm so excited for you that I can hardly contain my joy from bubbling over. I openly share this time-tested, surefire, and effective program with you because these are the very steps which I created and utilized to recognize and marry my very own *soul match* (I am having a ball and so will you)! Not only has this Biblically-based, yet practical, relationship program worked for me, but it has also worked for a wide variety of women, who just like you desired and deserved to have and enjoy real love with a well-matched mate. I've taken special care to specifically arrange each chapter to effectively take you from the initial "How do you do?" to the matrimonial "I do."

This first chapter will help you to solidify your self-perception and self-worth. The second will show you how to avoid the disrespectful "unequally-yoked" *deadweight date* and instead reserve yourself for your delightful, decent *heavyweight mate*. Next, the third step will help you to examine and evaluate your concept of and readiness for "real love" and a life of "togetherness" and "forever."

Once you complete and determine how serious you are about meeting your soul mate, the fourth step will take you by the hand through the process. Thereafter, Chapter Five will show you how to bypass and redefine the usual dating phase, and instead create purposeful, platonic and non-sexual dating where you use your discerning spirit and intuition to "interview" and uncover the person's true intentions and compatibility level. Once you get into Step Six, you will be shown how to enter into monogamous courtship with your compatible mate, where you will "try his spirit" before you both fall deeply in love. Finally, Chapter Seven will show you how two souls can recognize and bond together through the power and presence of the Holy Spirit, practical application, unwavering belief, perseverance, prayer, and some good old-fashioned courage.

Are you ready to take your wedding stroll down the aisle to be bonded with your sacred "Mr. Right?"

Say Goodbye to Romantic Guessing and Hello to God-Centered Blessing!

This manual will help you to remove the false beliefs that there aren't any marriageable men available, and not enough good ones to go around. Nonsense! Keep in mind that you're not looking for a series of men to "go around." With this spiritually-sound program, you are going to meet the compatible match for you. All it entails is for you to recognize "the one" that God has already made specifically with you in mind (and for your soul mate to recognize you also).

With God, there is no guess work, no coincidence, no on-and-off luck, no happenstance, no probability ratio. There are precise and on-target blessings. God removes the guessing and replaces it with purposeful blessing!

By following this program, you will never indulge in any reckless relationship game or any emotional roller-coaster ride with any unsuitable character who may want to drop in your life for a quick recess and then do a disappearing act. You no longer have to ever play musical chairs with your emotions, where you're the only one left standing without a chair when the music stops playing.

You are worth too much for any hit-or-miss relationship selection. Do you really know how valuable you are? You are specially crafted by a loving God, who created your spirit, molded your soul, formed your body and even numbered each strand of hair on your head. How special you are!

Psalms 139:14 records how wonderfully, preciously, and purposely made you are. Therefore, walk in your blessings, and select a wonderfully and purposely made soul match. It is your natural birthright to enjoy healthy love.

The key thing to remember is, if you're looking for a *Prince,* then you can't entertain and kiss *frogs.*

Here's why:

Dear Dr. Grace,

I have just finished reading your book *The Band-Aid Bond*. Thank you for your passion for empowering women to live their potential. My reason for writing to you is two-fold: I want to express my thanks, but I also needed to vent – you know, get some things out. I think you are amazing and the work you do around the country with women and men is more than commendable.

I am a 34-year-old, divorced woman. On the outside, everyone thinks that I've "got it going on" (I make a generous salary, I own my own home, and am financially secure). [But] nothing could be further from the truth. I am a complete mess. I had a physically and emotionally abusive husband who I left six years ago, only to get involved with a con-artist. He was handsome, charming and talented. He was also a womanizer, a liar, and a manipulative ex-convict. All the signs were there from day one, but due to my low self-esteem, I felt honored that someone so handsome would even take an interest in me. I endured three years of neglect, emotional abuse, and financial ruin. But I was so convinced that I loved him and couldn't live without him, I stayed. Truthfully speaking, the only reason we are not together right now is that he is back in jail.

From there, I had a string of one-night stands, and one night "friendships," where I traded sex for companionship. I felt like I wasn't worthy of anyone loving me, so I just did whatever it took not to be alone all the time, although most of the times I was.

I do very much want to get married, but how do I know my husband won't cheat on me like my ex? I know you're very busy, but if by some chance this e-mail does reach you, please pray for me, because I don't know how (or what), to pray for myself.

Chelsea

From past grief,
to joyous relief!

Dearest Chelsea,

If only you had realized how valuable you were in the past relationships, you never would have put up with the horrible and disrespectful behavior you accepted. But let's pick up your self-esteem and turn your past grief into joyous relief. Sometimes when you get disappointed by a divorce or when the trust is broken from a former relationship, it emotionally trips you on your life's path. There is nothing wrong with falling down, as long as you can get back up, look at the dirt as a learning experience, brush yourself off, and form an honorable agreement with yourself that you will never allow anyone to ever trip you again by having so much power over your heart and better judgment. You've been looking to feel loved and lovable again. That's quite okay. What's not okay is, you've been selling yourself short by looking for love in the wrong places and in the wrong faces. The first place you have to start is in your very own heart, and the first face is the one staring back at you in the mirror.

You have to start
with your very own heart

It is not easy to do this when people have taken you for granted and have trodden all over your self-worth; however, take heed to this profound truth. No one has the power to abuse, confuse or misuse you, unless you stay in the situation. The world is full of many unscrupulous con-artists who will attempt to use you, but you don't have to accept their advances or behavior in your life.

Stop handing the management of your life and self-worth to unsuitable and shady characters. You are much stronger than you are giving yourself credit for.

Embedded within your very center is the power to accept only kind treatment and reject all evil and mean-spirited individuals. This wise Biblical truth is found in Luke 10:19 where the Lord says, "I give *you* authority over *all* the enemy, and nothing [or no one] shall harm you."

Realize how valuable you are. My dear, you are a unique treasure. You are a beautiful, exquisite, hand-crafted couture gown, specially designed by a loving Creator. Don't diminish your worth by getting involved with a back-street, five-n-dime, off-the-rack, unsuitable tailor. You are *falsely overestimating* the con-artist's importance, and *wrongly underestimating* your own. It is time to flip the script!

Stop idolizing people by thinking they are better than you, no matter how handsome, rich, or athletic they may appear. You have been too hard on yourself. You do deserve to have a healthy and sacred love and marriage with someone perfect for you who will not mistreat, beat, nor cheat on you. But first you have to really believe that you are worth it (and you truly are). As far as being able to trust again, it takes time to peel away the various layers of hurt that have worked their way into your heart. But I assure you there are many trustworthy and decent men who are single and available. Don't buy into the myth that all men cheat – it just isn't true.

There are <u>four types of men</u>:

1. Some cheat when they're young, but stop when they're old (or become mature).

2. Some never cheat when young, but start when they're old (when the mid-life crisis kicks in).

3. Some never stop cheating (dysfunctional personality disorder).

4. But a whole lot never, ever start cheating either (they make excellent husbands)!

You have to decide to turn over a new leaf in your volume of life and not allow anyone to smear or crumple your pages. Choose wisely. I prayed for you before I wrote this letter. My prayer for you right now, as you're reading, is this:

May the presence of the Holy Spirt of God enfold you with comfort,

may He embrace you to His bosom and just rock you gently,

may you know how valuable and worthwhile you are,

may you understand why He took time out to make *you*,

may you walk in your purpose and your blessing,

may you experience peace of mind and simply take a moment to *breathe* – just stop for a moment and – *breathe*.

May God truly bless you. You really deserve to know your true worth. To help you tap into your inner essence, I've attached a special list of "10 Commitments" for you. I created it for my inspirational seminars and included it in one of my previous books, *10 Bad Choices*. It will help you to realize that you do deserve to be treated kindly.

Claim it,
Dr. Grace

THE TEN COMMITMENTS
"A Time to Be Kind to Me"

1. A time to stop beating myself up about my past life and past mistakes. A time to say I've made mistakes – and so what? A time to move forward.

2. A time to stop condemning myself – to stop criticizing and belittling myself. A time to stop feeling insecure and bitter about what I don't have and to start counting my blessings for what I do have.

3. A time to groom myself properly. A time to make myself as healthy, clean, and pretty as I can with what God has given me.

4. A time to be truthful with my thoughts. A time to be bold and not be afraid of speaking my mind or showing my true feelings.

5. A time to stop letting others take me for granted. A time to stop giving away my talents for free. A time to appreciate my creativity.

6. A time to appreciate the beautiful body temple that God has blessed me with, even though others may fail to do so. A time to know that I am a lovely gift from God.

7. A time to know I am worthy of love. A time to let only a nice, decent man into my life. A time to know that my sexuality is valuable. A time to know that I'm important – and allow myself to love and be loved.

8. A time to get rid of negative energies. A time to have only good friends who genuinely care about my well-being. A time to remove all the deadweight from my life.

9. A time to say, "Too bad for what others may think of me." A time to make me into what I think I should be. A time to commit to becoming the best I can be.

10. A time to just smile and welcome joy into my life. A time to just be kind to me.

(AMEN)

I pray that you are also ready to welcome joy in your life. This is your time to enjoy the better and avoid the bitter bonding. We must learn to listen to the still, small voice within that instructs us in each choice we make and each step we take. In Exodus 19:5, God said, "If you will hear my voice, I will make *you* a peculiar [special; unique] treasure among many, because all this world is mine." The Holy Spirit is always there whispering caution to us in each situation.

Here is an example of someone who, after much trials and tribulations in her early childhood, and much heartache in her young adulthood, learned to get in touch with and locate her God-given purpose. She is now on a new path, preparing for her sacred match:

A time to avoid the *bitter*,
and attract the *better* bonding

Dear Dr. Grace,

My name is Victoria. I live in England. I am a 25-year-old, single mother of one. You don't know what you've done for me. I know you may not get to read or reply to my mail, but telling my testimony and blessing will do me the world of good. I need to tell it; I can't keep it in! That is what happens when the Lord above blesses you (something I'm quite sure you know about).

I was raped at eight years old by a stranger. I was forced into an abortion at 21. Then, at age 22 I got pregnant with my son. I was again asked to abort (by the same guy), and I said, "hell no!" I was left on my own to look after my baby. I have been used and abused emotionally by men. I have only had two sexual partners. I was in one of the relationships you described in *The Band-Aid Bond,* where the guy says you're friends, but wants your body. I let it happen. I have been to hell and back.

But, after all [of] this, God placed me in a spot where I would realise that men can't fix me and that I should stop asking and expecting them to. He then took every single little piece of me and mended me back into the strong woman that I am today. Your books reinforced what the Creator made of me, and I want to say thank you!

I know that I was placed here for a reason and I have recently found it. I also know that I am ready for healthy, sacred love. This morning I prayed that God would send me "my husband," and I know he's on his way to meet me (thank you). I ask that you please find a moment to pray for me on my path to new heights.

I've photocopied and framed the **"Seven Sacred Self-Nurturing Sentiments"** from your book and have placed them on the vanity next to my bed. I read and affirm them along with my prayers every night before I fall asleep and every morning as soon as I wake up. Please keep writing, and whenever you come to London, please let me know, as I know I have much to learn from you still.

God bless you,
Victoria

Dear Victoria,

I'm so very sorry for what you experienced as an innocent, young child. I'm filled with joy for you that you have made an intimate connection with your Creator and have developed such a healthy sense of self. I prayed deeply for you and, while I was praying to the Lord asking how best I could assist you, this came to mind:

Clean out the old to make room for the new

This is a special message which I shared with tens of thousands of women in my inspirational talk around the country called, *It Couldn't Touch Your Soul!* I also shared it with thousands of readers in *You Deserve Healthy Love, Sis!* I'd like to share it with you in this letter because I believe it will help you to peel away the emotional band-aid covering the wound of childhood molestation, and begin a permanent healing process:

**It Couldn't Devour You,
So It Helped To Empower You**

"You are here today for a special reason, for a mapped-out purpose. You've been through quite a lot – a lot of awful, cruel, and hard experiences, but you made it through. You are still here (hallejuliah)! You made it through for a reason. It should have never happened to

21

you: it wasn't your fault; it wasn't your fault; it wasn't your fault! The corrupt creature overpowered you, took advantage of you, frightened you – he hurt your body; he hurt your mind; but his cowardly act *could not touch your soul!* The demonic energy (spirit) that drove that individual to rape, molest, abuse, and overpower you and had stolen part of your innocence, had taken many joyful years out of your life, had come to hurt and destroy you. But not anymore!

"You are still here because you are here for a purpose. *It couldn't touch your soul!* It has harmed your flesh, brought sorrow and fear to your mind, broken your spirit...but *it couldn't touch your soul!* It couldn't take you out of this world, because *you* are here for a purpose. Your soul connects you to a oneness with God, and no one, no energy, no spirit, whether natural, supernatural, or unnatural, has the power to harm or take you out if you know how to surround yourself with the armor of God."

The Bible instructs us in Ephesians 6:13 to "Take unto you the whole armor of God, that ye may be able to withstand the evil day, and having done all, to stand [firm]." What was meant to destroy and devour you, God turned it around to strengthen and empower you!

You are on the right path and God will indeed bless you with the right one – soon!

Much blessings,
Dr. Grace

Here are the "Seven Sentiments" which Victoria referred to:

Seven Sacred Self-Nurturing Sentiments

1. I will not doubt or belittle myself about former choices and past mistakes. I refuse to keep looking backward and be governed by situations that were or those that "could have been."

2. I free myself from negative thinking – I now focus on each of my blessings and give thanks to God for both the great and small wonders.

3. I look in the mirror each morning and greet my own reflection with my best smile and compliment, "Girl, you've been through a lot, but you're still here. You're looking good, and getting better and better each day!"

4. I attract fantastic people in my life who are kind, compassionate, honest, and respectful of my ideas, time, and value.

5. I am capable of making the best choices for my own life because I am blessed with a discerning spirit and a keen intuition.

6. I feel dynamic, terrific, and attractive, and I love being me!

7. I realize that I am a gift from God and I wouldn't trade myself for anyone in the world; today is a new beginning and I embrace each moment with hope and faith.

Like Victoria, you may have been weeping and lamenting long enough – this is now your time to dance, to smile, to embrace – it's simply *your* time to love!

> To every thing there is a season, and a time to every purpose under heaven: A time to weep and a time to laugh; a time to mourn, and a time to dance...a time to embrace...a time to love.
> (Proverbs 3)

Spiritual Truth # 2:
"Be Not Unequally Yoked"

> ## AVOID THE *DEADWEIGHT DATE*;
> ## ATTRACT THE *HEAVYWEIGHT MATE*

You are on a path towards meeting and marrying your true soul mate, you definitely cannot afford to slip into the grip of anyone who is psychologically or emotionally unhealthy or spiritually and physically unclean. This is so important that the Bible warns and instructs us in 2 Corinthians 6:14 not to be "unequally yoked."

There are a lot of people who have years of self-mending to do because of the emotional wear-and-tear of being involved in unhealthy, unbalanced, unproductive, and unsuitable personal relationships.

The purpose of this chapter is to help you remove the mask and see the true intentions of any would-be player. You have to be able to discern the spirit within the package of each individual. Many times people come wrapped in beautiful, attractive outward packages, but are filled with ugly intentions, personalities and behavioral patterns within. All that glitters isn't gold, it could be shiny brass, which will eventually tarnish on you. In Matthew 23:27, Jesus spoke boldly about how people can be deceitful and hypocritical and "appear beautiful outward, but within are full of uncleanness."

If you truly pray from the heart, the Holy Spirit will open a deep spiritual awareness within you that will prevent you from being involved with any unclean con-artist like this woman was:

Hello Dr. Grace,
Your books have gotten me through some very difficult emotional times and I thank God for you and your wisdom. I'm positive that He is inspiring you. I need your help with a relationship issue. Last year, I met a man (who approached me). On the first night we met, we ended up talking until five o'clock in the morning while walking in the park. We had a lot in common, exchanged numbers, and he asked me not to forget about him. He made the comment, "You know how you meet someone that you really seem to hit it off with, then you never hear from them again? Please don't do that to us." He called me that same morning because he wanted me to see where he lived. He invited me to his home. I went. He showed me around, we talked more, he wanted to have sex, but of course I said no way (although I was tempted). I left after making plans to talk later that day.

**Start with his inner heart,
not his outer body part!**

We started dating and he asked that we date each other exclusively. He had filed for divorce and showed me the papers, so that I wouldn't think he was lying. He treated me very well, but it was obvious that he had some emotional issues to deal with. And, as time went on, I also suspected some sexual addictions (porn/voyeurism), and mental issues as well.

Pay attention to your intuition

He seemed to be stuck in his past, often bringing

up things from his first marriage in 1975, and the most recent one which he was ending in 2003. He has a very kind, gentle and loving heart, but a seriously messed up head. Or, as my Godmother has stated, "Honey, he sounds like a good person, but a little touched in the head!" I would have to agree, but I try to look at the positive side of all situations. I know that I am not perfect and also have some emotional demons to overcome, especially when it comes to trust. I got down on my knees when I first met this man and asked God to guide me because I did not want to be hurt again. I needed God to direct me on how to deal with the things that I saw which could be potential problems in our relationship. He is also very difficult to communicate with because instead of facing the true issues at hand, he reverts back to past incidents, or just shuts down. I know that there is no way we can move forward, or grow in communication, if he does not open up honestly.

He decided to end our relationship seven months ago, after saying that he couldn't deal with us "arguing" (Dr Grace, we have never argued). So many times I wanted to talk with him about my fears and concerns, but I held back. He refused to tell me this lame reason until a month after we had been apart and I was in emotional limbo. As I cried in pain, lost 20 lbs, and was once again emotionally devastated, I continued to pray, asking God to PLEASE remove the pain. Since every woman before me had left him (I can understand why), I promised that I would not leave him unless God showed me that he was not the one for me, or if he told me that he did not want to be with me. He attended church, spent time with his nine-year-old son every other weekend, during which we did family activities together (my children really like him).

He began to call me again three months later, using the excuse that he left a photo at my house. After three more weeks had passed, he finally told me that he missed me and the intimate times we spent together. He said he wanted to work on our communication and let things move at their natural pace, but not be boyfriend/girlfriend. We started spending time together again and things have been going great until this morning (which is now two and a half months later). This is what finally led me to send you this e-mail, which I intended to send months ago.

When I stood in church last Sunday, I placed him on the altar in prayer as I prayed for us and God's guidance in this relationship. After spending a wonderful night together, I woke up before he did. As I lay next to him, I was thinking about where we stood in regard to our relationship, and if he would ever get past his emotional and other demons. His phone rang at 6:30 am, but the answering machine picked up. What I was feeling as I lay next to him was fear of being hurt again, pondering if he would do the same as before – just ending our relationship out of the blue. So, I got up and began to wash a few dishes that were in the sink as I thought about this.

He came into the kitchen and asked me what was wrong. When I began to tell him that I was afraid of being hurt again and mentioned the phone ringing so early in the morning (suspicions of another woman calling), just as it had in the past, right before he ended our relationship, tears began to roll down my face. He got angry with me, stated that he thought we had talked about this, that we were not boyfriend/girlfriend, that we would take things slowly, and that he didn't want to rehash or go back to the past (referring to the last time I broke down and was trying to get him to talk to me).

I explained to him that I am a woman, I am emotional at times, and that I had a lot of things that I have been through that I had not shared with him yet, and still had a lot of pain inside my heart. He still just shut me out and when I was attempting to explain to him what I was feeling, he wouldn't even look at me. He kept his back turned to me as he ignored me, pointed towards the door, and started telling me about his schedule for the day. I had to beg him to walk me to the door. I kissed him as I left crying, and wondering if he would even call me again.

Dr. Grace, what happened? This is the same man that spent over $300 to send me to the Day Spa for my birthday eight months ago; the man who told me he really appreciated me listening to him as he shared some of the things he was going through; the man who held my hand as we walked for hours through the park. I understand that he still has some healing to do in regard to his ex walking out of their relationship (even after they had attended counseling together and he proposed to her at church in front of the whole congregation). He also said he liked the fact that he felt that I let him be himself without judging or belittling him.

I am so tired of just wanting to be loved for who I am, but not feeling truly appreciated for the times that I am understanding of what's going on with him. I am tired of riding what you described in *The Band-Aid Bond* as an "emotional roller-coaster," when all I want is to be LOVED! I have decided to just stand still, pray, and wait on God's direction and strength, and praise Him while I wait. I'm going to give this relationship some space. I don't know if he will call again, or if I should call him after some time has passed.

Do you have any advice that you could give me at this point because my head and heart are both hurting from trying to figure things out? May God send a special blessing your way for the help that you have given so unselfishly to others.

Thank you for your time,
Stacey

Head before heart to avoid falling apart

29

Dear Stacey,

You have been through quite a lot of disappointment and dishonesty. It's okay to want to be loved – you should be. However, you were unequally yoked in a mis-matched union. A word of caution: Never, ever enter into any relationship by trading sex in hopes of getting a commitment in return. You are too valuable to freely open up your body temple to any unsuitable character. The man that you described sounds as if he has a major personality disorder or an unclean spirit. Whichever condition he's suffering from, he needs serious help, especially if your suspicions of "porn addiction and voyeurism" are involved.

Honestly speaking, I receive a lot of letters from women who have contracted Sexually Transmitted Diseases from being involved with men who are sleeping with multiple people. Instead of wondering whether or not he'll call, or if you should call him , I suggest you unplug from the chaos and thank God (really thank Him), that you did not end up contracting AIDS or some other STD from being intimate with this unsuitable character.

I'm going to keep it real and be up-front with you. If anyone ever approaches you with a "sex first" relationship, tell him to keep on stepping – don't fall for that ridiculous request, no matter how lonely you may feel. In all relationships "keep your mind open and your legs closed." I know this is a straight-forward statement, but trust me, I'm tying to keep you from years of heartache and future pain. I get approximately 300 e-mails every week and most of the letters are from women who were entangled in ill-fitted relationships.

Let's take a candid look at your situation. After he left you the first time, then decided to return for another "trial run," he did tell you that he didn't want to be involved in a "boyfriend/girlfriend" relationship. Unfortunately, you both incorrectly crossed the proverbial friendship line by sleeping with each other. It was a game to get you in bed without accountability on his part – and unfortunately, it worked for him. And when you finally gathered enough courage to confront him with the truth, he disrespectfully dismissed you – so why do you still want to subject yourself to this? Think about it, is he really worth it?

If it doesn't fit,
why force it?

Let me use an analogy to get my point across. Have you ever suffered from wearing tight, ill-fitting shoes? What a horrendous experience – you can't think properly! Just about every part of your being suffers from the affliction and pain the ill-fitting shoe is causing you – your head hurts, your teeth, your ears, your ankles, your toes – you are completely agitated.

When you get involved with a mate who isn't the proper fit, who isn't the right one for you – even if you believe that in time, he'll eventually stretch to suit your needs – you are setting yourself up for great discomfort and pain. Two of the major causes of pain and breakups are incompatibility and unrealistic expectations. Don't try to make him into something he refuses to become. You saw the early warning signals when your intuition – your spiritual voice of reasoning – revealed to you that he probably had some form of "sexual addictions." Then your wise godmother confirmed your suspicions of dysfunction, by revealing that although he "may seem nice, he may also be a little touched in the head."

Unfortunately, many women go into relationships with the notion that they can "fix" the man's failure to commit. When he fails to do so, they devalue their own self-worth and deem themselves unworthy. What's really unworthy is the incompatible, uncomfortable, and unsuitable fit. If someone refuses to make a monogamous commitment with you, then accept it. Don't force him into something he may not be capable of, nor interested in doing. That may not necessarily make either of you bad people, you're just a bad fit – you don't belong together – that is not your soul mate. You are a worthwhile individual who deserves to be loved completely and unconditionally. Don't waste your precious time and emotions trying to change or "stretch" the wrong man. Instead, concentrate on becoming the best *you* that you can be. Conserve your energy, self-respect, and precious body temple for the right, mature, willing and decent mate who really wants to be with you exclusively. Trust me, once you meet him, you won't have to sit by the telephone wondering if he'll ever call – you'll know that he'll always be on call just for you. Why subject yourself to the pain and disdain of ill-fitting shoes? Let go of the torture – shop wisely for a comfortable pair!

Wishing you the very best,
Dr. Grace

Examine Your Fears:

Hindsight is always 20/20. It's easier to examine a situation when you are emotionally removed from it. I hope that Stacey's story will help you to avoid being emotionally entrapped in a tumultuous affair with someone who doesn't have your best interest in mind. Ask yourself, what makes you stuck on this particular person? Is it really about who he is, or more about the fear you feel?

Are any of the following fears holding you emotionally strapped to a counterfeit relationship?

1. You've been celibate for a while and you're just tired of being single.

2. You are getting anxious because you're getting older and feel your biological clock is ticking away.

3. He's the first guy who has approached you in a long time.

4. His professional credentials are impressive on paper.

5. He's really good looking and attractive.

6. He has money.

7. He keeps pursuing you.

8. You've already slept with him.

9. Your family and friends thinks he's a good catch.

10. You just simply want to be married!

Does any of the above apply to you? If yes, which ones, and why? _____

_____

_____

_____

_____

_____

_____

Keep in mind that it's quite normal and natural to want to meet your very own Prince Charming, but take your time and choose wisely so you won't end up with a Prince Harming in disguise.

Be Smart With Your Heart
...as sheep in the midst of wolves; be ye therefore wise as serpents, and harmless as doves.
(Matthew 10:16)

It is no secret that there are quite a few wolves parading in sheep's clothing who travel recklessly through life dipping in and out of as many women's heads and beds as they please. It frequently happens that a woman may share a thorough discussion with a man about wanting a committed relationship, and may either prematurely assume or be falsely led to believe that he is on the same level, but in time, the hidden truth surfaces, and she finds out that it was all a disguise so he could have a physical fling.

Realistically speaking, the world has always had many irresponsible Casanovas who prowl around, trying to wolf as many women as they can. Sadly, it always will. But *you* must take the full responsibility to be smart with your heart. Deuteronomy 30 talks directly to us about making wise choices each and every day: "I set before you this day life and good, death and evil, choose life that you may live [joyfully]...the word is in your heart that you may do it."

It can be painful to let go of unhealthy choices once you've invested your emotions, but believe me, it's not as painful as remaining in additional years of misery with an unequally yoked cheater.

Here are some useful tips from an article in *JET* magazine (July 2004). It's entitled: *Dating 101: How to Spot a Cheater.* It shows how to avoid being caught in a deceitful net:

Watching how a person interacts with others is one way to spot a cheater, says psychologist Dr. Grace Cornish, bestselling author of *The Band-Aid Bond: How To Uncover the Hidden Causes and Break the Pattern of Unhealthy Loving.* "If someone openly flirts with others when they think you are not looking, that's an early tip-off," says Cornish, a noted relationship therapist who has offered her expert advice on numerous TV talk shows. "Not all flirters cheat, but that's an early giveaway."

Looking into a person's eyes, she adds, can also help you spot a cheater. "The eyes are the windows to the soul. Some people are notorious liars and can look you in the eyes. But the eyes always give you away. Someone can tell you one thing and do something different.

"Be careful if someone's eyes are darting all over the room." Cornish says people should watch how people interact with you in regards to others. "If someone is constantly spending time with their 'friend' and never introduces you to that person and introduces you to others as a 'friend,' that's a major tip-off." Those who constantly accuse you of cheating, says Cornish, may do so because that's what they are guilty of doing.

"If a person is always accusing you of being unfaithful," she explains, "they are trying to make you so self-conscious that you won't look at what they are doing." A person's telephone etiquette, Cornish says, can also signal a cheater. "When the telephone rings and the person answers in a whisper or turns down the ringer when you're over their house, that's a clue. Or if the person takes the phone into another room. And if they say 'me too,' that's a dead giveaway that someone said 'I love you' and that person is responding."

If a date refuses to give you a home telephone number or home address, she says, that's a big red flag. "A P.O. Box will not substitute," she states. "If a person refuses to give you a home telephone number, that's a problem. What are they hiding?"

Don't waste the *right* feelings on the *wrong* fellow

Good question – what are they hiding? But more importantly, why does the woman stay, even when she knows he will stray? If there is any unhealthy relationship you need to sever the ties with, but you can't seem to make a clean break, set some time aside to evaluate what is holding you captive in a non-win union. Very often, many women use the right emotions, but too often on the wrong men.

The following should be reserved for your perfectly-matched soul mate. If used in the wrong relationship, it can blur your better judgment:

1. You're mesmerized by how wonderful it feels to "have a man."

2. You spend most of your time fantasizing about all the exciting things you can do as a couple, that you couldn't do on your own.

3. You mentally rehearse how you'll permanently share your life and lovemaking together.

4. You experience "butterflies in the belly" excitement by being swept away by his appeal.

5. You feel like dropping everything and spending all your available time with him.

6. You spend hours trying to find the right sentimental gifts, cards, or songs for him.

7. You re-do your closets, wardrobe and lingerie drawers with the type of clothes you think he'd like to see you wear.

8. You spend hours picturing the fantasy wedding of a lifetime.

9. You fantasize about having his children: how many and how they will look.

10. You plan your future on growing old together as his exclusive Mrs.

These feelings are fun and heart-warming for your spiritual Prince Charming, but can be distressing and damaging when used on the free-wheeling Court Jester. Let's take a look at this young woman's dilemma:

I was invited to be the relationship consultant for an article entitled "Relationship Make-over" in *Honey* magazine (May 2003). The case study I was asked to analyze was of a 22-year-old young woman named Natasha, who candidly shared, "I always seem to go after the bad boys I know will eventually leave me! I need a guy who can handle me – who can match the aggressive and dominant parts of my personality. But these guys are usually players, and I end up getting hurt. What attracts me to men I know are wrong for me?"

Honey magazine reported:

Natasha's pattern is all too common, says Grace Cornish, Ph.D., author of *You Deserve Healthy Love, Sis!* "Women [often] bypass nice guys and go for smooth-talking womanizers," says Cornish, who honed in on Natasha's [false belief] that she needs a man who can handle her – but points out that the opposite is true. "In reality, she's trying to handle him. Subconsciously she's thinking, 'If I can get him to commit, I will succeed where other women have tried and failed.'" But it's a loser's game. Here's how to break the player habit:

❶

•**Write off your Mr. Wrongs.** Cornish advises Natasha to catalog her past relationships and write a brief summary of why she was drawn to each guy and what went wrong. Then she should list all the things that each of these men failed to bring into her life that she deserves, and finally, list everything she wants from a relationship and a man. "Seeing in black and white the ways she's keeping herself from a good relationship should really hit home," says Cornish.

➋

•Take a man break. Cornish suggests that Natasha steer clear of men for at least three months – it takes 21 days for the brain to begin forming a new habit. In the meantime, Natasha should do things solely for herself – exercise, take a foreign language class. She needs to appreciate herself alone before she can attempt a healthy relationship with someone else.

➌

•Set up a lifeline. To make sure Natasha sticks to the new pattern, she should ask a caring, nonjudgmental friend to be on call and set her straight if she starts to slip. "Sometimes all we need is a reality check from people who care about us and keep us on the right track," Cornish says.

●

The following checklists will help you to draw a clear demarcation between a responsible suitor and an irresponsible user. I created the list some years ago for my national relationship programs. It has already successfully helped thousands of women to make better choices and was originally published in *10 Bad Choices*. I've modified it for you as follows:

The 12 Disadvantages of *Dating a Deadweight*

1. He is constantly "between" jobs and never working.

2. He asks you for loans, but never pays them back.

3. He never pays for dates, even when he invites you out.

4. He dictates how you should spend your own money.

5. He asks you to buy him gifts, yet never buys you any.

6. He expects you to pay his bills.

7. He takes your *kindness for weakness.*

8. He always finds ways to *take away* your best.

9. He tells you how lucky you are to have him.

10. He is a "walking liability" who always holds *your* own.

11. He seeks *sex before commitment.*

12. He constantly strays.

The 12 Advantages of *Having a Heavyweight*

1. He has his own satisfactory job.

2. He has his own bank accounts and balances his own checkbooks.

3. He always pays for dates when he asks you out.

4. He does not interfere with how you spend your own money.

5. He buys you gifts, yet never pressures you into buying him any.

6. He pays his own bills.

7. He takes your *kindness as sweetness*.

8. He always finds way to *bring out* your best.

9. He tells you how lucky he feels to have you.

10. He is a "walking asset" who always holds *his* own.

11. He seeks *commitment before sex*.

12. He constantly prays.

Now that you know the difference between a spiritually clean heavyweight and an unscrupulously tainted deadweight, pay close attention to God's instructions in 2 Corinthians 6:17 "Come out from among them and be ye separate, saith the Lord, and touch not the unclean thing." In a nutshell, "Lose the user and choose a champion!"

Spiritual Truth # 3:
"Ask And It Will Be Given To You"

ARE YOU READY FOR "TOGETHERNESS" AND "FOREVER"?

This chapter will help you to evaluate if you're truly ready for "togetherness" and "forever" by guiding you to probe deeply and answer what *sacred love* really means to you. One of the key components of everlasting love is *balance*. As assuredly as the spiritual "ground is leveled at the foot of the Cross," so must both people be balanced at the heart of a sacred bond.

When you ask a woman what would be her ideal mate, she is more than likely to have a very specific list of attributes. She usually wants a tall, handsome, rich, intelligent, spiritual, respectful, educated, witty, capable, and strong man of a particular background and position. There is absolutely nothing wrong with this if that's her personal preference; however, each woman must be prepared to also be equally yoked and bring something of value to the table in her personal relationship. When you ask the same woman what she will offer her "specific" mate in exchange, she usually answers "me."

"Me" is a vague and unspecific answer when you line it up against the characteristics and fringe benefits that she is seeking. I am in your corner, cheering you on to set your standards high, but you must evaluate yourself and be prepared to bring balance, compatibility and a similar or equal level to what you're seeking in a mate.

Take a look at this situation:

Dear Dr. Grace,

I know you receive thousands of e-mails and I know you can't possibly answer them all, but maybe just getting this on paper will be therapy enough for me. I met you when you spoke at a conference in San Antonio recently. While you were signing a copy of *The Band-Aid Bond,* I got a chance to speak to you briefly. I told you that I had met a really nice guy and that I was afraid because it felt like he could really be "the one." I wanted to speak to you more, but I couldn't hold up the line because there were about 500 more women waiting behind me to have you sign their books also. You were so gracious; you gave me a warm smile and told me that *Chapter 8: The Emotional "Wear-n-Tear" of Lingering Fear* would help me to deal with overcoming my personal fears. You were so right and because of that, I have gathered enough courage to write this e-mail.

Dr. Grace, I have struggled with this for quite some time now. I love the Lord and have been celibate for fifteen years and trusting God that the next man that I am with will be my husband. I have been faithful and truly desire to be in God's will. This man is a great guy and he truly loves me. When I met him, he did not have a relationship with Christ, but the Lord would not let me stop communicating with him. However, he loved God, and has now accepted Jesus as his savior. He attends church with me, but he is not spiritually mature in the things of God. He says that God sent him to take care of me. He is wonderful in doing that.

A few years ago, I was diagnosed with chronic arthritis and he has been very supportive and helpful when I'm in pain, and her truly takes care of me. I've been unable to work full-time due to my illness, and he's always there for me, financially and emotionally. He is sensitive, kind, and communicates his thoughts and feelings openly. I prayed for a man that would be able to communicate and share his thoughts, a man that would love me as Christ loves the church, and someone that would love my children (I have teenage twin boys from a past relationship), a man after God's own heart. I love to have deep conversations, and so does he.

Now, this is my dilemma: We are engaged and plan to be married in June. Dr. Grace, I have waited patiently for the man God has for me. I am 40-years-old and have never been one of those women that desperately wanted a man. I have been content where I am. I just knew that God had something special in store for me. I have been keeping myself for my husband, but I recently fell short in that area; I slept with my fiancé. I had sex with someone for the first time in fifteen years. I truly love him and know he loves me. He is a good man, but my guilt is eating me up.

When I asked God for a husband, I prayed that he would be well-endowed [with a large penis]. I had a very fruitful sex life when I was in the world and I know I want to be faithful to my husband. Dr. Grace, this great guy is *not* good in bed! It was awful. He is not well-endowed and does not satisfy me physically. I don't know who to talk to or who to trust with such information. I believe I sinned and that is something painful in itself, and I gave myself to someone, and to find this out [the size of his penis] is devastating. I thought for a moment that it was terrible because we were engaging in premarital sex. He knows that he does not satisfy me sexually and we have been able to communicate openly about it.

Please hear me in the spirit. It seems that all my girlfriends that have man-hating spirits [who male-bash] meet such great guys – financially, spiritually, and physically. I don't understand why God would allow me to fall in love with someone that doesn't have the physical and spiritual levels I want. Don't get me wrong – I know God gives us choices. And, I always ask God to reveal this man's heart, and pray if this was not the man for me, to please remove him from my life because I don't want to be out of God's will. Every time I did that he would say or do something that I thought was confirmation that he was the man for me. Even when I met you when you were signing my book, you said, "Write to me, because he could be 'the one' for you." That was one of those times when I was truly seeking confirmation about this man.

I gave him another chance and we have been together for eleven months. I have never been so confused and afraid in my life. Confused because I truly thought this was God-sent, and afraid because I don't want to miss God's blessings by marrying the wrong person. I have only felt this kind of love once in my life. This man truly loves me and I do love him. But, why the doubt? For the first time [ever], I've tried to look beyond looks, status, finances, and see substance in a man. He has inner qualities that I desire and that's what I fell in love with. I just can't comprehend what God is doing in my life right now.

I'm an interior designer and I haven't been able to draft any designs in over a year because of the arthritis in my hand, so I'm struggling financially, and have been gaining an extreme amount of weight. I say all of this because the area of romance seems to be the only beam of light for me right now. He is so kind and loving {he has also given me a beautiful engagement ring}, yet I don't know if this is the right guy for me. Forgive me for rambling on and on, but I have no one to talk to right now. I'm usually the one in the group that everyone comes to for advice and they just can't comprehend me ever having a problem.

The other thing with my girlfriends is, they are not happy for me. Every other word is, "Now that you have a man..." or "I want to meet someone like your man" or "When is God going to send mine?" They chorus this in an envious tone, instead of just being happy for me and rejoicing with me. I just needed to get this out. When I met you at the conference, I thought you were the most beautiful person both inside and out. I have never really seen a woman radiate beauty the way you do. I immediately felt a spiritual connection to you when you said, "Don't be afraid and don't throw away a good man." I've prayed about it and he kept coming back.

If you ever have the opportunity to write back, I would greatly appreciate it. It hurts beyond imagination. I cry out to God and I haven't heard anything lately. I just can't imagine marrying someone that I am not compatible with sexually. I can't imagine that after being celibate for fifteen years that I fell and it was not worth the fall (please forgive me, I just have to be real about what I am feeling). I truly love him and believed that he was finally it. Thanks for talking with me when you came to San Antonio. I tell all my girlfriends to get *The Band-Aid Bond* because it's truly liberating and has helped me to be open with my fears.

Waiting to hear from you,
Darlene

Explore the "test" hidden in your testimony...

Dearest Darlene,

First, let me thank you for being so honest and open with your personal situation. You are engaged by a "beautiful ring," but not necessarily by your heart's total conviction to marry this man yet. Sacred bonding is not about the aesthetic beauty of the engagement or wedding rings, but more so about the deep connection the "marriage" rings represent. Those two sacred circles are symbolic of a lifetime of unbroken love that connects two souls together. If one of the two souls is hesitant to walk hand in hand with the other, then it is possible that they are not soul mates, but instead, two mismatched souls temporarily mating – buying time – until either or both wake up to the reality that they have not yet found 'the one.'

Of the thousands of letters I've received and personally answered over the past fourteen years, I can honestly tell you that this is the first time I was lost for words regarding a personal relationship issue. To put it frankly, the reason why I was baffled for a moment was because I have never heard of anyone specifically praying to God to ask Him for a husband with a "large penis." I was really shocked because I couldn't believe that someone actually asked God about the size of someone's genitalia. I didn't know how to answer your letter, or even if I should. But I was so surprised by your specific and unusual request, that I read the letter again. Then I prayed about it before I answered you.

This is what was revealed to me: Maybe God is testing you — testing you to see if you are able to love unconditionally and uncompromisingly. Maybe He found your personal request to have too much emphasis on the sexual and not enough focus on the essence of what true love is really about. By going to God in prayer, requesting a special mate with a specific anatomical size, is probably telling God that you need to learn about the real meaning of intimacy. Not the physical intimacy (which is causing you to second guess this man's worth), but the spiritual intimacy, which on a deep level means: "into me, *you* see." Ask God to remove the scales from your eyes for a moment, and try to look deeply and really *see* this man's essence. You sound like you have a gold mine right in front of you, but cannot recognize this sacred soul because you're judging him by *what* he has (or doesn't have), instead of *who* he is.

I believe what's causing a lot of this confusion is the self-inflicted guilt that's eating away at your conscience for believing that you've "fallen and sinned." That's something personal that you should have a heart-to-heart talk with God about. It's not my place to either condone or condemn your and your fiancé's physical union because had he been as "well-endowed" as you had prayed for, would you be expressing these feelings of guilt, regret, and remorse, or would you be happily planning your wedding at this very moment? You have to examine and evaluate the depth of this relationship and what it really means to you.

Get to the heart of the matter – look deeply into whether or not you're staying with him because you feel guilty that you've already had sex with him, or are you planning on leaving him because you don't enjoy having sex with him. Whichever way you slice it, sex seems to be the deciding factor in your relationship. It seems that the physical aspect is overruling all other aspects of your relationship. Don't let this be a stumbling block and trip you on your path towards sacred love.

Let me talk with you on a higher spiritual level for a moment. Deep sacred relationships are beautiful, caring, and loving, but surface physical unions can become destructive, harmful, and ugly. They are complicated at times because they involve two individual, separate minds. Success depends on both people coming together in one accord – you are no longer in your individual worlds, you have merged with another human being and a new world, a new bonding now exists. This matrimonial sacred bond is repeatedly described in the Bible as "two [individuals] becoming one."

People are never the same during or after any relationship, because we begin by forming our relationships with our own sets of beliefs, then along the way, the relationships form us. At the beginning, only our boundaries (surface thoughts) meet, we reserve our interiors (our souls) from each other. Then, when we progress deeper, closer, and become more spiritually intimate, eventually who we really are (our sacred centers) start to merge.

When two souls blend, there is a new creation. This is similar to the two natural elements of hydrogen and oxygen. On their own, they are both valuable and useful, but when they blend, a new creation, water, is formed. It is the water, the healthy bond between hydrogen and oxygen, that quenches deep thirst. So it is when two souls blend; it is their sacred bond that brings forth deep love to fulfill their thirst for unconditional oneness.

When unconditional love is experienced, you venture deep beyond the physical periphery. You travel intimately towards each other's soul and become so consumed with the essence of each other that your physical forms are not hindrances, but instead, fringe benefits in your union. The relationship then becomes more meaningful, more spiritual, more fulfilling. All negative criticisms, false pretenses, unrealistic expectations, and shallow preferences are removed. You simply blend together.

My question to you is, are you really ready for a soul match, or are you more concerned with the size of this man's genitalia? Before you make a rash decision, examine all the facts – evaluate exactly what you are *both* bringing to the relationship. You say you love him also, but do you love him completely, or just love what he can do for you? You have someone who is in love with you, who takes care of you, and who above all, respects you. I understand your concerns, but take a look at the entire picture, your fiancé cherishes you and doesn't complain and criticize you for having a chronic illness, which you have no control over. Then, won't you extend the same understanding, patience, and love to him for having a body part, which he has no control over?

Examine your true motives. You say you are in love with your fiancé, so let me ask you this – if he were "well-endowed" and you had been married for years or even a short while, and for some reason he became ill, and unable to perform in bed, would you leave him, like you are considering doing now? What if he were to take on that mind-set and leave you because of your condition? Think about it – that wouldn't be unconditional love, would it? That's why it's important to evaluate yourself to find if you're really in love with him, or just involved with him because you're tired of being alone. There is a major difference between being *involved* and being *in love*. Make sure you examine the difference. Do you see where I am going with this line of reasoning?

Of course you should be attracted to your mate, especially if you plan to spend the rest of your life with him. You must be able to enjoy each other in *all* aspects. However, don't simply base your entire future on his physical performance (or lack of it) in bed. Get to know his *sacred center* first. Trust me, couples can always find creative ways to spice up their love life and marriage because "the marriage bed is undefiled." (Take a look at *The Song of Solomon* in the Bible and expand your imagination.)

The real test of unconditional love is examining the person's overall essential character and not just his physical characteristics alone. The ultimate decision is *yours* to make. But I strongly advise that you pray about it deeper, ask the Holy Spirit to give you clarity, marry this wonderful man who absolutely adores you (then you will have released your guilt, your body will be more relaxed, and you can *make love* with each other, not merely have *sex*), and you'll be surprised how both of you can find creative ways to spice up your love life together.

I'm really convinced that once you're able to pass this test, and look deeply into his eyes, and realize just how much you love each other, one day you'll look back, and wonder, "What took me so long to embrace his soul?"

Sincerely,
Dr. Grace

Seven Irrational Reasons To Rush In:

Before you read any further, take a deep look and make sure you're not entertaining the idea of marriage for the wrong reasons. Let me emphasize a profound truth that I came up with while I was writing *The Band-Aid Bond*: **Marriage is a personal choice in loving, not a public requirement for living.**

Take a few minutes to think about this. Under no circumstances whatsoever should you let anyone, any situation, or any guilty feelings make you feel pressured to rush into a marriage. Make sure you're not doing it because of false beliefs and other people's expectations. In the same regard, please do not string anyone along if you have no true intentions of ever marrying them.

The following are seven unhealthy reasons to prematurely dash into an engagement en-route to marriage with anyone. Don't rush in because:

1. You are longing for a ring on your finger.

2. You feel that your biological clock is ticking.

3. Your family and friends are pressuring you to.

4. You feel you have to 'hook' him before anyone else does.

5. You feel he owes you for all the years you have already invested in the relationship.

6. You want to be addressed and labeled as Mrs. So-and-So.

7. Your friends are getting married and you feel left out.

ASK:
Are you really ready for *real love*?

Here's an excerpt of the Biblical definition of *real love* as found in first Corinthians 13. The following is an exact recording of verses 4-8 in the New International Version (*NIV*):

> Love is patient, love is kind. It does not envy, it does not boast, it is not proud. It is not rude, it is not self-seeking. It is not easily angered, it keeps no record of wrongs.
>
> Love does not delight in evil, but rejoices with the truth. It always protects, always trusts, always hopes, and always perseveres. Love never fails.

Answer these honestly:

1. Is there a time when I may have turned away a potentially good relationship with a man because I was not ready to let him into my life? If so, when? What would I change about that situation today?

_____

_____

_____

2. If a good man came into my life at this very moment, would I feel ready to receive him? Why, or why not?

_____

_____

_____

3. Do I define a man's worth by his career, position, possessions, education, salary, physical attributes? Why, or why not?

_____

_____

_____

4. Are there any personal emotional blockages that have hindered me in a past relationship? (i.e.: guilt, anger, resentment, fear, embarrassment, feelings of inadequacy) If so, what are they?

_____

_____

_____

5. Do I believe that any man really deserves me? Who or what type? Be honest with yourself...

_____

_____

_____

6. Am I open to the possibility of joint decision-making at this point in my life? Why, or why not?

_____

_____

_____

7. Am I flexible enough to learn and grow with a mate, or do I picture him in a specific role? Why, or why not?

_____

_____

_____

8. Do I feel uncomfortable when someone does something nice for me? Why, or why not?

_____

_____

_____

9. Do I believe that I am worthy of being treated kindly? Why, or why not?

_____

_____

_____

10. Am I suspicious of a man if he tries to compliment me? Why, or why not?

_____

_____

_____

11. Are there any specific situations that I would like to act over in my life? If so, what are they? What would I change? What would I say and do differently?

_____

_____

_____

12. Am I who I want to be? Explain.

_____

_____

_____

_____

_____

_____

_____

_____

_____

EXAMINE YOURSELF:
"Leave no stones unturned"

I want to get married because

_____

_____

_____

_____

_____

_____

_____

_____

_____

_____

_____

_____

_____

_____

_____

EVALUATE YOUR VALUE:
Ask the "big" question

This is your chance to be very specific about your special qualities. Write about yourself. Include at least 10 wonderful things about you. Don't hold back – be confident with your personal characteristics and worth. When you know who you are, you will not look at another person to complete you, and will not be upset at him for not having all the items on a preconceived list. Evaluate your value, so you can effectively share it in a beautiful, assertive, kind and non-threatening manner. Go for it!

What value can I give to (share with) my specific soul mate?

_____

_____

_____

_____

_____

_____

_____

_____

_____

_____

_____

_____

Now that you know your value, let's continue to the next chapter which will show you where to meet potential suitors... Ready? Let's go...

Spiritual Truth # 4:
"Seek And You Will Find"

EXPLORING THE BEST PLACES TO MEET A DECENT MATE

It is alleged that in North America alone there are over eight million more available marriageable women than there are available marriageable men. If we were to attempt to meet and marry a man based on the psychological, emotional, and physical aspects alone, we would be playing a hit-or-miss guessing game because the statistical figures just wouldn't add up.

However, let me share the good news with you. When you add the spiritual aspect to the equation, you will attract admirers on a higher level who would love to meet you. God can readjust and turn statistics around in your favor. I don't believe in luck, coincidences, or odds, especially when it comes to people's lives and their spiritual and emotional investments. I believe in the Holy Spirit's blessings, coupled with a discerning spirit and a practical approach, so you, yes *you,* can choose or refuse in a manner that's pleasing to God.

The purpose of this chapter is to inform you where to meet available and decent potential suitors, and to enable you to become more approachable in a non-threatening manner. It was once believed that the best place to meet a good husband was in church.

Church is an excellent place to have pre-marital counseling, but as far as your chances of meeting your husband you must keep your options open. Let's be realistic and do the math; in most churches the ratio of women to men is generally 70% to 30%. However, with the current growth in male spirituality, the gap is narrowing to an average of approximately 60–40, at best.

Most married couples did not meet in church. So don't be discouraged if you've not met your perfect match in your congregation as yet. Although my husband and I are both Christians, we did not meet in church – actually, he walked right up to my front door – talk about on-target blessings. (I will share the exciting details with you in Chapter 7.)

In the meantime, I want you to keep in mind that you can meet decent men anywhere. You're not looking for quantity, you are to seek quality. So, in that regard, there is no shortage for you to be worried by. Unfortunately, most women have given up hopes of ever taking their matrimonial stroll down the aisle because of negative and untrue beliefs that they are limited to meeting their ideal mate within the confines of their immediate vicinity, community, or place of worship.

Take a look at this example:

Dear Dr. Grace,

I have enjoyed reading your books, especially *The Band-Aid Bond*. Please keep writing wonderful self-help books. My name is Jacqueline. I'm divorced and raising two sons. It took me more than seven years to get over my ex. I love going to church and I give God all the praises for helping to raise my boys, and for giving me life abundantly.

The reason why I'm writing to you is, I believe I deserve to be with someone who is nice, generous, affectionate, has good manners, and is a good person in general. I've been celibate for six years and I'm scared to blend back into the dating scene. I am a nice, kind-hearted person and a good mother. I did not get married right the first time. I got married to my son's father (because I was pregnant), after my first son was born. So if I ever get married again, I'm going to make sure I do not have sexual intercourse until after I am married.

I live in the Mid-West and there are so many want-to-be players who want to fool women. As a child, my grandmother took me down South and taught me how to be a lady with good manners. Of course, as I got older, I forgot all that early training, but now, I'm going back to church. I attend church regularly. I've been in this church almost two years, but they always have retreats for married couples only – never anything for the singles in the church. I'm thinking of switching churches again because, how can you cater to couples and forget about the singles? We pay our tithes just like everyone else. I have voiced my opinion on this twice – once in the suggestion box, and recently in a survey.

I just want someone to love me for me. I pray all the time for God to send me someone. I'm not a gold-digger and I won't mess with married men. Please write me back and let me know how do I go about meeting someone who cares about me.

Jacqueline

Dear Jacqueline,

I understand your frustration and concerns regarding meeting someone who is interested in a monogamous relationship that leads to marriage. Each year I conduct a Top-Ten List of where happily married newlyweds meet. The most recent was of 300 couples who were married within the last six months. The results are as follows:

The Top-Ten Places To Meet A Mate:

1. Work (a two-way tie with School)
2. Homes and gatherings of mutual friends
3. Special-interest classes
4. Conferences and conventions
5. Church
6. Social and community events and activities
7. Gospel concerts
8. Public transportation (train stations, bus stops, airport terminals)
9. Libraries, bookstores (museums)
10. Weddings

After reviewing the list, you'll get an idea that you can meet decent and available men anywhere. There are thousands upon thousands of marriageable men everywhere – although all you need is one. Pray and ask the Holy Spirit to help you recognize and decipher your particular soul match from the masses. Your aim is to find one good man, who is not only good for something, but also good *to* you and good *for* you.

One basic ice-breaker is to simply smile and say a friendly hello to every man you encounter in a safe environment who you are reasonably sure is not a felon, a fanatic, or an atheist. Many women feel uncomfortable initiating the first hello because society has conditioned us that it may not seem proper for a woman to pursue a man. But here's the thing – you are not pursuing anyone at this stage, you are simply exchanging a cordial "hello" that may lead to a pleasant, platonic, non-sexual, and non-threatening conversation. Speak to each man with the same courtesy, respect and warmth as you would when meeting a woman and discussing a shoe or pocketbook sale with her. Try it and see.

Men are not strange creatures. Remove the mask of mystery. Don't be influenced by the "Men are from Mars, Women are from Venus" hype. The simple truth is, we are both human beings, equally created by one God, to occupy planet Earth together, until His appointed time to disrobe our coats of flesh and move us through His spiritual door. So don't give anyone the power to either make or break you. Respect each man, but worship none.

Here's an insider's secret for you which I was told by countless men in my national study groups: Most men are afraid of rejection – no man wants to be rejected. So the same way you're wondering what he's thinking if you say hello, he's pondering the same notion about you also. That's why a warm friendly smile, whether in church, a social club, a library, or at a conference, may give him courage to approach you with a decent hello and begin a conversation about the weather, the environment, the Bible, or just traffic. If you choose to, you can start a friendly conversation as you would with your very own brother. Learn how to have healthy, unattached, non-sexual male friendships.

Here's food for thought: There may already be one particular guy or a couple of possible suitors who greatly admire you and would like to speak to you, but because you may not seem approachable, they could be hesitating to even say hello in fear of being ignored or rejected. (You may be the most wonderful, sweetest, and caring person on the inside – but don't sell yourself short by hiding your sparkle from the rest of the world. Make sure your facial expression reflects your inner beauty with a pleasant smile.)

Hey, you never know who's admiring you in your office, from pews in Church, at your neighborhood businesses, at your gym, or just anywhere safe. Keep your options open. Remember to form genuine friendships. I've attached a exercise for you that will help you to examine your beliefs and become comfortable with having a friendly conversation with the opposite gender.

> May God open the way
> for you,
> Dr. Grace

Here's the exercise I sent to Jacqueline. Try it and test your friendship factor. By the way, when I refer to "friend" I mean exactly that. I know some women sometimes cross the line and use the term "my friend" to define a man who they are sleeping with but who has not clearly made and developed a committed monogamous relationship with them. Don't fall for this trap – it really is defeating and ridiculous – that's not friendship. That's a fling or an affair.

Avoid the trap
with the "bed buddy" chap

A friend is a buddy who is like a brother, not a "bed buddy" who you may secretly be tip-toeing through the tulips with. If you're caught up in a situation where you're allowing a so-called "friend" to string you along and use you, stop fooling yourself that everything is hunky-dory. It won't be when the "hunk-y" walks out of the "door-y" and leaves you in emotional limbo, sad, and sorry. You are worth so much more. If you are serious about being married, keep a clear definition, be honest, and cut the string with the "bed buddy" fling.

Evaluate your personal concepts and beliefs about having genuine, non-sexual male friendships.

EXERCISE: **Examining The Friendship Factor**

1. How do I feel about men and women being good friends? Do I believe the myth that the two genders can't be "just" friends? Why, or why not?

_____

_____

_____

_____

_____

_____

_____

_____

2. Does it seem unnatural or uncomfortable to picture myself in a platonic, unemotional friendship with a pleasant man? Why, or why not?

_____

_____

_____

_____

_____

_____

_____

_____

3. Do I currently have any really supportive male friends? Why, or why not?

_____

_____

_____

_____

_____

_____

_____

4. What are my greatest apprehensions and/or fears about having a friend who is a man?

_____

_____

_____

_____

_____

_____

_____

5. How would I feel about asking a man's advice about another man?

_____

_____

_____

_____

_____

_____

_____

6. If I had a good brother-friend as close as a best girlfriend, would I abandon him if people didn't understand our friendship? Why, or why not?

_____

_____

_____

_____

_____

_____

_____

7. Do you believe that men can be trusted? Do you trust your own feelings to develop a friendship with a male without *you* having any emotional ties or thoughts? Why, or why not?

_____

_____

_____

_____

_____

_____

_____

Here's a different approach to meeting a decent, spiritually-minded, suitor:

Dear Dr. Grace,

I would just like to take the time to tell you what an inspiration you are to me. I recently read your book, *The Band-Aid Bond* and I have to tell you I was blown away! I realized that many of the things that were covered in there applied to me. I am not one to follow a lot of advice that psychologists give, especially those that appear on television. It's just a bias of mine I guess. But you are so down to earth with a spiritual quality that is lacking in most psychologists, regardless of color. I've seen you on a number of talk shows throughout the years, namely *Queen Latifah* and *Ricki Lake*, and I was always impressed with your insight and warm honesty. You are one of the main reasons that I went into the field of psychology and a reason that I recently decided to place an emphasis on spirituality when I acquire my Ph.D. in Clinical Child Psychology.

I am 28-years-old, extremely lonely, and quite frankly frustrated with the dating scene today. The men that I meet in the city where I live are not interested in advancing themselves or interested in being in a relationship with a woman who is accomplishing her goals. They either go after the women with loose morals or they try to have a strictly sexual relationship with me. This is something that I will not tolerate or abide by. I try to go outside of my immediate environment and meet men who have the same interests or moral standards as I, but I have no such luck.

My friends and family say that I'm very pretty and I get lots of attention from men, but I would like a long term relationship that leads to marriage with a warm and caring man who is sincere, honest, and trustworthy – and yes, he has to be physically handsome (at least to me). But every man I meet is just not interested in [getting to know] me.

Dr. Grace, I know that you receive a lot of email. But I would really appreciate it if you would take the time to reply to this one because I have come to the point in my life where I realize that I need help – I am beginning to doubt my looks and my self-esteem. I'm a conservative dresser, not one of the flashy, movie star types. For starters, where do I meet decent men? I really value your opinion on this issue. Thank you and God bless you.

Monica

Dear Monica,

There is not a thing wrong with you – keep your head up. I'm going to keep this letter short because I think I have a solution that will help you tremendously. Normally, I do not recommend on-line dating services, but there is one in particular that has been creating quite a positive buzz. It's called *E-Harmony*. The website is www.eharmony.com. It's for everyone, but it is also very Christian based. It does a thorough screening process of all who log on and then matches you to potential suitors based on your profile. I've heard really good results from some women who've met their husbands through that service. Try it and let me know how it works out for you.

By-the-way, please do not doubt your looks or self-esteem because of past disappointments. Disregard and discard any myth or false belief that you have to look like a certain a movie star, magazine cover model, or advertisement pin-up girl to be admired. I have worked with quite a lot of actresses and models, and most of them don't look a thing like the fantasy image projected on the screen and in the pages of magazines when the makeup is off, the lighting is natural, and the airbrushing and computer generated retouching machines are absent.

Beyond all the glitz and glamor, they are real women – beautiful women, just like you and me. So don't let planned advertisement cause you to belittle your looks or body temple in any manner. Give yourself a natural facelift by lifting your spirits with a smile. You'll be surprised how many people will come up to you and want to be in your presence.

Keep smiling,
Dr. Grace

A decent man will sooner approach someone who he finds warm and pleasant, than one who emulates a stoic, untouchable mannequin. Trust me, this works. When Richard and I first met, it was totally unplanned. I was completely natural and casual. I was wearing an oversized T-shirt, sweat pants, flip-flop slippers, no make-up, reading glasses, hair clean, but slightly disheveled, accessorized by a pleasant, genuine, bright smile. As he tells it, he was immediately drawn to and attracted by my smile and bubbly personality. He said I reminded him of "a beam of sunshine on a cloudy day."

In all honesty, if the truth be told, meeting men is not a problem. The challenge is what do you once you've met them. Let's go to the next chapter and see...

Spiritual Truth # 5:
"Knock And It Will Be Opened To You"

OPENING THE DOOR TO PURPOSEFUL DATING

Once you've met and formed amicable non-sexual friendships with some decent and upstanding men, you can determine if there is anyone you would like to date. Keep in mind, *dating* means *communicating*. (No emotional involvement in this phase.) It doesn't mean *relating* or *mating*. Relating will be further discussed in the following chapter when we look at how to move from dating to *courtship*. Courting is dating with a purpose – that purpose is to help you recognize and marry your very own soul mate.

There are some women who men *wed*, and others who they only *bed*

Now, let me say this about *mating* – Your body is a temple and what you do is strictly your personal decision. But realistically, there are some women who men *wed* and there are others that men only *bed*. If you're tired of all the old game-playing and dishonesty, then refuse to be used anymore; your aim should be to remain or become the type of woman that your ideal mate will both wed and bed. Make sure you know where you're heading before you get to the bedding. In other words, no monogamous contract, no sexual contact. Let him first prove that he's worthy of you.

The purpose of this chapter is to help you find out whether a potential suitor is worth your time and attention to move from *the dating stage*, to *the courting stage*, and then to *the matrimonial stage*.

In order to effectively move from one stage to another, from the "How do you do" to the "I do," you must pay close attention to early warning signals.

Dear Dr. Grace Cornish,

My name is Virginia. I'm a 22-year-old, hard-working, determined to succeed, single mother of a four-year-old child. I am currently not in a relationship, but would eventually like to be in one. I can't say that being alone is definitely by choice because when I meet someone I'm interested in, they naturally assume that I already have a boyfriend, no matter if I tell them I don't. I really don't know if that's just their way of not moving into something more serious with me, or just an excuse to only be involved in something sexually, if I give them that opportunity.

I have come to realize that a lot of guys nowadays (at least in my age range), only want sex. I want to do what's right and that's why I read books like *The Band-Aid Bond* and more self-help books that will help me to make better decisions regarding possible mates. When I finish reading these books they make me feel alive and refreshed. I agree with, learn from, and try to follow the advice throughout the books. But, then it seems that reality hits when I pull my head out of the book and the same old "all I want is sex" men are still out there. And, they are ready to walk right by if you aren't "giving it up."

I've only been in one real "relationship" and it was for four years. I was 16 and he was 18. I learned a lot from that one relationship, and vowed that I would never be that gullible again. I try to pay attention to the early warning signals that a person sends off that might do me more harm than good. For example, when I meet someone I listen for key words they say about their joy, living situation, or even if they continuously talk about an ex-girlfriend.

I don't want to go through a lot of drama and I don't want to keep giving my body away to anyone who isn't going to stay. But when I let the men in my life know that I don't want anything sexual, they act as if they understand, but then they walk away. And if I do sleep with them, they still leave. It's like you're "damned if you do, or damned if you don't." I just don't know what to do. At this point, I believe I may just be single for the rest of my life at this rate. Dr. Grace, I would really appreciate some sound advice.

Please help,
Virginia

"Patience is a virtue"

Dear Virginia,

Don't get discouraged, believe me, you are not "dammed" as you mistakenly believe. Meeting and recognizing the right man for a serious courtship that leads to marriage takes patience, time, effort, and honest prayer (and believe me, it's worth it once you've recognized each other). You are on the right path by weeding out and avoiding all the sex-driven predators and reserving yourself for your true decent love. Unfortunately, we often encounter a whole lot of unsuitable *frogs*, before meeting the compatible *prince*. You no longer have to go through the disturbing "drama of giving your body away in hopes of getting them to stay," as you candidly shared. My advice to you is never give up hopes of ever finding your true love, but keep examining early warning signals as a guideline to avoid being tricked into a no-win situation.

Pick wisely, choose properly, and refuse coherently

To find the right person for you, you need to make good use of your abilities, talents, time and value. Since it is not humanly possible for you to sift the men you meet through a giant colander, you must use the wisdom of the Holy Spirit to sift them through your life by first learning about them, them separating the wheat from the tares, and in this manner, you can pick wisely, choose properly, and refuse coherently.

Make sure you don't ignore the selection process and rush blindly into an unrestrained physical fling anymore. You are much too valuable for this. At 22-years-old, you have an entire lifetime to meet some decent suitors. You are way too young to throw in the towel on the hopes of ever finding healthy love. Take some special interest classes at a local college or university campus, go to church, attend museums, or gallery openings to meet a new level of decent men. Form platonic, non-sexual male friendships. Go out together. And if and when you start to discuss dating, then you can help to keep the dating stage refreshing by recommending a variety of interesting activities as you get acquainted with each other.

Whether you live in a big city or small town, you can include many attractions such as places with historical interest, sightseeing tours, boat or helicopter rides, fishing, mountain climbing, or just sitting by a lake.

Here are seven activities that can spark decent and worthwhile conversations between you:

1. View your city from the top of the tallest buildings, or visit the oldest structures in your town.

2. Go to your town or city center to find out its history and take a guided tour.

3. Visit a TV station and sit in the audience at a live taping.

4. Go to a newspaper plant and ask for a tour to see its operations.

5. Visit an automobile museum, car show, old railroad station or railroad museum.

6. Go to an antique furniture shop, attend an auction, or an estate sale on a Saturday afternoon.

7. Visit a science museum or attend a lecture on a topic you both enjoy.

> Keep in touch and let me
> know how you're doing,
> Dr. Grace

The following charts will equip you with the necessary know-how to examine some of the early warning signals Virginia referred to. Pay attention to the individual's behavior in the *Diagnosis Evaluation*, and then compare it to the matching number in the *Prognosis Analysis:*

DIAGNOSIS - EXAMINING EARLY WARNING SIGNALS

If he does this:

1. He flirts excessively.

2. He refuses to communicate about his past or family background.

3. He sees a "friend" or an ex regularly without ever inviting you.

4. He doesn't like to discuss his deep feelings with you.

5. He believes that he should always be the sole decision maker.

6. He drinks very often.

7. He insists that you have to let him know your every move.

8. He acts distant and doesn't seem to care for you as much as you care for him.

9. He's stringing you along and refuses to discuss marrying you.

10. His favorite conversation and main topic is <u>always</u> about sex.

PROGNOSIS - ANALYZING "THE PROBABILITY FACTOR"

It probably means:

1. *He's probably* a cheater (he's definitely disrespectful).

2. *He's probably* concealing very important and serious issues from you.

3. *He's probably* still being intimate with her.

4. *He's probably* emotionally-unavailable.

5. *He's probably* a control freak.

6. *He's probably* a border-line alcoholic.

7. *He's probably* obsessive and possessive.

8. *He's probably* doesn't want to get too close to you.

9. *He's probably* commitment-phobic.

10. *He's probably* a sex-addict.

If any potential suitor displays any of the prognostic characteristics – then *he's probably not* looking for a serious relationship and *definitely not* worth going into the courtship stage with. Don't blur your vision with rose colored glasses, ask the Holy Spirit for a vivid spirit of discernment so you can see each prospective suitor for who he is today, not who you hope or wish he'll become tomorrow or change into someday. Don't ever get involved or become attached to anyone because you feel sorry for him or believe you can change him.

This dating stage is your opportunity to evaluate each man's character, personality, and availability. If you are seriously looking to get married, then don't simply date just for entertainment, diversion, or pleasure seeking, like a lot of people mistakenly do. Use this time wisely to get to know *who he is* and *what he stands for* before forming a courtship.

When a man considers marrying a certain woman, he usually evaluates and analyzes her as a prospective wife from the early dating stages. He may not pop the question by the third date, but believe me, he knows whether or not a woman is *marriage material* or *mistress material* by then. Make sure you set the standard right from the beginning by reserving your emotions until you're sure that he's *husband material*.

What exactly is husband material? You'll have your own definition of course, but here's a good basic guideline:

"S" MARKS THE SPOT:
12 SPECIAL QUALITIES OF "HUSBAND MATERIAL"

He is:

♡**Spiritual.** He believes in, respects and loves God.

♡**Sincere.** He is kind, compassionate, and considerate of your feelings.

♡**Sweet.** He respects you and really cares about your well-being.

♡**Stable.** He is dependable and loyal. He is not a womanizer. You don't have to worry about him being fickle or cheating.

♡**Sensitive.** He is emotionally open with you. He's strong enough to share his fears and his feelings with you. He's not afraid to cry in front of you.

♡ **Single.** He is available. He is not already in a relationship with another. He believes in monogamous unions.

♡**Straight.** He is not a closet bisexual or homosexual man. He is a truly heterosexual male.

♡**Supportive.** He appreciates your worth and wants the best for you. He encourages you to follow your dreams and ideas.

♡**Stimulating.** He is a good conversationalist. He keeps you mentally interested and challenged. He likes to learn and share new things with you about life. He's optimistic, not pessimistic and dreary.

♡**Sensuous.** He is romantic, charming and attractive. He is appealing and has excellent hygiene. He is clean, smells good, and grooms himself well.

♡**Smart.** He is an intelligent and creative thinker. He is sensible and self-aware.

♡**Successful.** He has his own job and he does it well. Whatever position he holds, whether he owns the boardroom, runs the boardroom, or sweeps the boardroom, he makes an honest living and keeps himself out of debt.

In the dating stage, you must put your best foot forward and let each potential suitor know, in a pleasant and charming manner, that you are no frivolous, fly-by-night, fling, but instead a warm and beautiful woman who expects to be treated with kindness and respect. If you date with a clear purpose, within the first three dates you'll both know whether or not you'd like to see each other on an exclusive basis, which will then begin your monogamous courtship.

It's better to have a few good quality dates getting to know a potential suitor, than a large quantity of dates with meaningless conversations that take up unnecessary and precious time. A good tip is to avoid spending your dating stage going to noisy events, concerts, movies, sports, or the theater. You'll have plenty of time to enjoy these amusing activities once you move into the courting stage. You should spend time having worthwhile and enjoyable conversations, whether you are having a picnic lunch, going for coffee (or tea), a business lunch, or a mid-morning brunch at a restaurant or at a family diner.

CONSIDERATE COURTESIES, ETIQUETTE, AND DATING ECONOMICS

Call me traditional, or even old-fashioned, but I don't believe women should pay for dates. However, once you decide to enter into courtship with each other, then by all means, you can offer to contribute or pay for some of your outings together.

With that in mind, let's be realistic, dating can be very expensive. A considerate courtesy for you to extend is to also accept invitations where a potential suitor can spend worthwhile time in healthy conversation with you at moderate or no cost. So whether he takes you to a fancy, expensive restaurant or a simple neighborhood café, maintain a pleasant and consistent decorum. Even the wealthiest of men appreciates a woman who is respectful of his earnings and doesn't come across as a high-maintenance date who is more interested in the contents of his wallet than the content of his character.

Once he opens his soul to you, he will gladly shower you with both love and luxury. At this stage you want him to invest his undivided attention and show his true self by freely talking openly and comfortably about himself. Remember your aim here is to get to know him. He will want to spend time with you again and again once he feels comfortable opening up to you, and at the same time, you will get information about him, directly from him, to decide if this is someone you'd want to spend more time getting to know.

Here are 3 Considerate Courtesies:

1. Be considerate of his finances, the same way you would with a close girlfriend, co-worker, or relative.

2. When you're at a restaurant, don't order the most expensive thing on the menu just because you can – order a moderately priced dish that you will enjoy.

3. If you are out with him, and you run into someone you know, introduce him courteously and proudly.

While you're enjoying your telephone conversation, meal, afternoon stroll, or trip to the museum together, make sure you interweave these pertinent questions into your early acquaintanceship:

KNOW BEFORE YOU GO COURTING:

1. What is his full birth name?

2. What is his date and place of birth?

3. Who are his parents or relatives, and where do they live?

4. Where does he work?

5. Where does he live?

6. Who are his friends and companions?

7. Has he ever been married before? If yes, is he legally divorced? For how long, and why?

8. Has he ever been arrested or had any legal troubles? If yes, what for, and why?

9. What are his beliefs about violence and infidelity?

10. What are his humanitarian beliefs?

11. What are his religious beliefs; does he have a personal relationship with God?

12. What are his beliefs about dating vs. courting?

Here are *The 7 Significant Knows* and *The 7 Mandatory Nos* to keep in mind:

The 7 Significant Knows:

1. *Know* if he's single and available.

2. *Know* what are his spiritual beliefs.

3. *Know* what are his beliefs about monogamy and infidelity.

4. *Know* what are his beliefs about violence and anger.

5. *Know* his home number (his cell, work, mobile, and beeper numbers are not to be used as substitutes).

6. *Know* his home address (no P.O. boxes; and if there happens to be a roommate for any reason, make sure it's not a "bedroom mate.")

7. *Know* if he's currently working; if he enjoys his work and can hold onto gainful employment.

The 7 Mandatory Nos:

1. *No* babbling on about or belittling an old relationship.

2. *No* acting like a movie character, soap opera actress, or one of your girlfriends just because they always seem to have dates. (It's not about the *quantity* of dates, but about the *quality* of each individual.)

3. *No* forcing yourself to emulate a certain image you assume he'd want you to become.

4. *No* concealing your true personality and beliefs (especially spiritual), because you are afraid that he may not like you for who you are.

5. *No* enduring disrespectful and/or foul conversation (let him know how you really feel).

6. *No* assuming that he's the right one for you without getting to know him further, and especially not without praying about it first.

7. *No* giving him your body trying to win him over.

Pay close attention to the last point, "No giving him your body trying to win him over." Here's an example why:

Dear Dr. Grace,

My name is Dawn and I live in London, England. I just finished reading your book *The Band-Aid Bond*. I have also read *10 Bad Choices*. I truly believe God directed me each time to get each of these books at the time I was going through something and was asking God to show me and help me to hear Him.

When I read *10 Bad Choices* it shook me and I applied myself accordingly, but I did not stick to it. But, Dr. Grace, this book *The Band-Aid Bond*, has really woken me up. What can I say but thank you, and I also thank God for you, and ask that He will keep on blessing you.

I was in a relationship with my children's father for about 20 years. I'm only 38-years-old, but look about 25-28, which I've been told by everybody. During this time we had separated; he went with someone else, we got back together, and I somehow became the other woman. I was in love with him, had his children, and thought it would be better to share him than not have him at all. It took a long time for me to come to my senses and realise that I deserved better than that.

What made me finally cut all emotional ties with him was meeting someone else; even though I have had other short-term relationships before, none of them could break the bond. This new man did that. I have only known him for a total of four months, but he made me feel special and loved. At first, he wined and dined me, always took me out, constantly phoned, and did all the chasing (pursuing). <u>But, then he switched as soon as I had sex with him</u> and started to really show loving and caring feelings towards him – then, I was the one who kept calling, telling him, "I need to see you, etc." It was deplorable, devastating, and nerve-wracking.

I realized from the description in *The Band-Aid Bond*, I had come across the "hit-n-run" and "bait-n-switch" lover (pages 31-35). When I read this, all I could do was laugh (with tears of joy and relief), because I already had shed a lot of tears of sorrow (and confusion). It was like you were writing about me – like you were a fly on the wall seeing and understanding everything. Because of your book and my prayers to the Lord most high, I have taken a definite stand. Even though in the past, we had said we would just be friends and hang out together, we still have been intimate.

Dr. Grace, this stops TODAY! God directed me to the book shop last Saturday morning and *The Band-Aid Bond* had just come in the same day. What does that tell me? I was meant to read the message in there because your book changed my life for the better! I'm God's child, my body is a temple, and now I know that I deserve better. I am now praying for and saving myself for my soul mate. I believe and I have faith that God will bring him to me soon.

With gratitude,
Dawn

Recreational Sex
will "Wreck" God's Creation

Good for you for letting go of those unhealthy sexual flings and realizing that you are a valuable temple of God. A lot of people drift aimlessly through life and various relationships, recklessly indulging in sexual intercourse as they would indulge in a typical recreational sports activity. You are on the right path, and I believe and will continue to pray that you and your soul match meet and recognize each other very soon. (Way to go Dawn!)

She made the wise decision to stay away from the deadweight date, and reserve her body for her very own heavyweight soul mate.

I was asked to be a consulting expert for an *Ebony* magazine article entitled, *5 Biggest Mistakes Sisters Make on Dates* (October 2003). The magazine read:

Introducing [physical] intimacy into the relationship too quickly may be the quickest route to the demise of a healthy long-term relationship. "It may be cliche, but if a woman sleeps with a man too quickly, he won't respect her," says Dr. Cornish. "And that's directly from the mouths of the many men I've talked to, researched and counseled. So, if he's worth it, let him wait."

My very good friend, fellow author and relationship consultant William July II, who was also interviewed for this article, agreed:

When sex is introduced into a dating relationship, it blows the dynamics off the scale. It is so powerful that it clouds all the issues. At that point, the sex becomes the focus, or a necessary ingredient, and it easily overshadows the process of getting to know each other. The couple will not get to know each other well enough to build a relationship, and what they do have may be short-lived," adds the author of the soon-to-be released, *Confessions of an Ex-Bachelor*. "The biggest mistake a woman could make is to allow a great date, or a series of great dates to make her starry-eyed and swoon to the point that she goes to bed with the man too early.

"Overall, what's most important to the success of any 'could be' relationship is a mutual desire on the part of each person to have a 'true' relationship.

"Both people must be committed to the idea of having a 100 percent participatory relationship," says July II. "Both must share the same values, structure and goals in the relationship."

You are worth the wait

Take heed and listen to the invaluable advice given from a healthy-minded male perspective. Continue to date with purpose and do not allow even the greatest date to leave you "starry-eyed" with blurred vision and assuming a monogamous commitment when it's really not there. When you meet your soul match, you'll have similar values and 100 percent commitment. He will respect, cherish and adore you. He will realize that you are special and worth the wait. I know first hand that it works!

Here's a portion of a *JET* magazine article entitled *Can A Couple Remain Celibate Before Marriage?* (March, 2003):

Relationship expert-author Dr. Grace Cornish and husband, research scientist Richard Livingstone, recently married [July 2001], but were celibate while dating. Cornish, whose new book *You Deserve Healthy Love, Sis!*, says that if a couple decides to be celibate before marriage, they must be honest with their reason why. "I know a lot of people who say they are celibate for religious reasons, but they are pretending," she says. "You have to be honest with why you are celibate or you will sneak and do things if you choose celibacy because a religion is telling you not to have sex without explaining why [It's a personal walk and decision for which you need a deep spiritual and profound understanding of what it means that your body is indeed a temple of the Living

God]. It comes down to your spiritual contract with God and where you are in your life.

"A lot of people end up in pain when they have sex before they know a person. Make sure someone shows you total affection [and matrimonial dedication] before getting into the physical part of it. You are worth the wait."

You certainly are worth the wait – especially in this day and age with rising AIDS statistics, unplanned pregnancies, and bi-sexual men coming out of the closet. Unfortunately sex-too-soon is a major stumbling block which catapults a lot of women into whirl-wind, counterfeit relationships with mis-matched mates. Many women get so caught up in wanting to be married for the sake of marriage, instead of for the love of finding their particular soul match, that they often pick, stick, and jump into bed too quick with little regard for their body as a sacred temple. Second Corinthians 6:16 reminds us of this universal truth, "*You* are the temple of the living God."

Don't rush into any pre-mature sexual en-counter with anyone, no matter how "wonderful" he may seem. Instead, get into your prayer closet, proceed with caution. Keep your hopes up, your dress down, and your spirit in tune to the voice of the Holy Spirit instructing you with that still, small voice to "look before you leap and *try his spirit.*"

Spiritual Truth # 6:
"Try His Spirit"

CHECK HIM OUT BEFORE YOU ENTER INTO COURTSHIP

Once you've made a commitment to date a certain man exclusively, you are now entering the *courtship stage*. This stage is dating with a purpose – that purpose is to recognize and marry your very own soul match. This courtship stage is a monogamous agreement to see each other exclusively. You are dating-to-marry and it's romantic, fun and soul-searching. At some point during courtship, you will be discussing marriage and future plans of living together for the rest of your lives. This is the falling-in-love stage and last phase before you get to the God-centered "I do." However, you must continue to look before you completely leap.

Ask yourself:

Am I attracted to the "person" or the "persona"?

Now you're equipped to weed out and avoid all types of unsuitable characters. In this stage you've narrowed your choice to someone who you believe is "that special one." But how do you determine if he's a good match for you? Even if you've started to fall in love with him, how do you know if he'll match your love equally and propose a life of togetherness and marriage? Here's a helpful hint: Before you start doodling and having fun writing your first name along with his last name, you must *interview* him for the position of your exclusive "Mr. Right" before you *audition* for the role of his one-and-only "Mrs. Right."

You must be sure that he will love you wholeheartedly before you completely open your heart to him. Take this brief three-question quiz to help you decipher whether this could be the ideal match for you.

How to know if he's the "real deal"

1. Does he enrich my life in any way?
2. Is he looking out for my best interest?
3. Does he like me for the individual I am?

If you've answered "yes" to all three, then he could very well be the right one for you. Next, determine if you are attracted to the person (kindness that brings joy to you heart, communication that inspires your mind, honesty that brings peace to your spirit), or the persona (the charm, the resume, his status, his position, his possessions).

Examine and answer each:

1) Can I comfortably discuss my/our religious and spiritual beliefs together?

If you're not on common ground with your beliefs about who and what God means to each of you, this will eventually cause a rift in your relationship. Don't try to conceal your true beliefs and hope that it will all just one day fall into place – it won't. Make sure you talk about your faith honestly and openly with each other. There's a wise adage that states "The couple that prays together, stays together." Start out on the right path – be sure to incorporate prayer in your daily life – whether together, or individually for each other.

2) Do we have similar interests?

You don't have to share the exact interests. As a matter of fact, having diverse preferences can help you to share new and exciting things with each other. However make sure you have at least a few common interests, so it won't be an ongoing battle over what to do and where to go to keep you both satisfied. You may have to compromise in some areas like sports, politics, movies, shopping, music, etc. Keep in mind that compromising doesn't mean depriving each other of their individual interests but instead, it means participating in each other's interests.

3) Do our personalities blend well?

Are one of you on the optimistic path while the other is on the pessimistic side of the track? Is one a spontaneous decision-maker, while the other needs advance time to let things settle in before coming to a conclusion? Opposites may initially attract, but eventually, they can repel each other. It's important that your personalities mesh. If one views life through rose colored glasses, while the other is always singing-the-blues, then you have to take a reality check.

Reality Check 101

Oil and vinegar may make an excellent salad dressing, but they don't mix well in romantic relationships, unless both personalities can find some sort of balance.

Evaluate what type of person he is: fun-loving, prankster, serious, laid-back, uptight. If you love each other's personalities regardless of any differences, and bring out each other's best when you're together, then this is a winning combo, and you could very well be a life-long dynamic duo!

4) Can you be your "true" self around him?

You are wonderfully and uniquely made by a loving Creator. If you find that you have to act or try to become someone you weren't born to be, just to be with a particular man, then something is seriously wrong. A true mate will appreciate you for who you are and what you are able to bring to the relationship. If you feel as if you're being pressured to alter your character and do things you wouldn't usually do (sex, drink, drugs), so that he will continue to see you, that's a certain sign that he's not the right one for you. Your true love will love you just for who you are – so don't be afraid, step out in faith and show your true self.

5) Can we relate and communicate with each other?

A soul match goes much deeper than a surface match. Even though you may both look good arm-in-arm, or standing next to each other whether in or out of church, can you talk when you're alone? What's going on in your conversations – are they deep and meaningful or surface and bland? Do you discuss your personal hopes, dreams and goals, or just talk about the weather, the daily news headlines, and the plot to the latest hit movie? Can you count on each other to lend a listening ear, good advice, and undivided attention? Good, honest and deep conversation will keep you deeply connected. When in doubt, talk it out. Always keep the lines of communication open in your relationship.

6) Do we get along with each other's friends and family?

Although the final decision of whether or not to couple has to be made by the two of you, some help from loved ones can be a major plus. Does he pass the test with your loved ones? Make sure you ask some supportive family members and/or closest friends their opinions about your choice. If the advice is not what you want to hear, examine it closely, evaluate the source, pray about it and make up your own mind anyway. But keep in mind that there is a chance that they could be seeing something that you're unable to see if you're "blinded by love." Let your head lead your heart, instead of the reverse. Make sure you also meet his family and closest friends to observe his interactions with them, and their interactions with each other. There is a wise old saying "Show me your company, I'll tell you who you are." An equally beneficial one is "The way a man treats his mother, is usually how he'll treat his wife." Evaluate the "family tree."

***Special note to you:** Although the advice of relatives and friends can be invaluable, the simple truth is some can become negative and overbearing if they are afraid that once you get married they may lose your company or your support. If you are facing unhealthy interference and discouragement from loved ones because of their personal insecurities (and not because of your mate's character), don't let them dissuade you. Instead, try to persuade and reassure them that you do love and appreciate them, but you also love and respect this man who could (or will) be your husband in the near future. Pray about it and make a decision that *you* feel comfortable with. Believe me, if he's the right one for you, he'll treat you well, and once your loved ones get over their fear of loneliness and personal deprivation, they will eventually accept him, regardless of their initial hesitation.

7) Do we laugh together?

This one doesn't need much explanation – if there's no joy, there's very little hope. Laughter keeps love alive. Find something that you can both get a good hearty laugh from. Here's a little secret that works wonders: A good sense of humor and a pleasant disposition has a magnetic attraction that makes people always want to be in your presence. How can he resist your beautiful smile and sparkling eyes? Have fun and enjoy!

So, how are you doing so far? Is there any particular area you need to work on? If there is, discuss your concerns openly with your beau. Make sure you get him to open up and talk. It is common knowledge that in general women talk much more than men. But, do you know that it is alleged that each woman speaks an average of 7,000 words every day, while each man generally utters about 4,000? Of course, with the Holy Spirit involved, worldly studies and statistics usually fall by the wayside and are of little or no value. However, let me share a little spiritual and practical secret here, if you can get a man to openly talk with you about his innermost feelings, dreams, memories, aspirations, and fears, you will gain his trust, warmth, and undivided attention. If you encourage him to share the events, situations, and experiences in his life which have had the most profound meanings and reveal his emotional center to you, he will develop uncompromising affection and a deep soul connection to *you.*

What will separate you – the soul mate (the soul connection) – from all the different relationships in his past or even his closest friends, is you will become an indispensable part of each other. You will become mirror images or "two souls reflecting one whole." You will talk your way in love with each other.

The key is to develop keen listening skills, by honestly paying attention to what he's saying. Learn about him, and in turn, reveal your true self to him. Here's a tip, once you're sure he's the right mate for you, then invest your time and emotions by encouraging him to be candid and talk openly about himself to you as if he were talking out loud to himself. Be the first to listen intently, because the one who listens first and speaks after, has the understanding of what the previous one said and can respond accordingly.

There's a wise old saying that "God gave us two ears and one mouth, so we can practice listening twice as much as we speak." This does not in any way means that you shouldn't speak your mind – you have to open up also. Just remember, your aim is to make him feel emotionally safe and spiritually comfortable enough to open his innermost center to you and just *talk.*

Richard and I developed a deep, meaningful, and spiritually-charged telephone courtship – we talked ourselves in love with each other. We made room in our very busy schedules to talk with each other every night over the phone for at least an hour or so. Sometimes we would spend all night on the phone talking away until the wee hours of the morning. We enjoyed talking with each other and looked forward to our daily ritual.

We talked about everything, and even in the busiest of times, we would take the time to say even a quick fifteen-minute, "I'm thinking of you; I wish you were here. May God bless and protect you." We knew more about each other within the first couple of months of our courtship, than some couples knew of each other who had been together for years. We used quality time wisely. Within three short months we knew that we would be getting married because our spirits were in one accord.

I'll share how the Holy Sprit connected us in one accord in matrimonial bliss in the following chapter. In the meantime, these thirty soul-searching questions are a springboard that will help your beau open up to you further.

Ask him...

1. What was he like when he was a little boy?

2. What are some of the experiences that he can remember before the age of 10?

3. How was he treated as a teenager and young adult?

4. What are some of his favorite and least favorite things about home and growing up? Which experiences would he like to relive, and which does he wish had never occurred?

5. Did he like school? What were his favorite subjects, hobbies, books, teachers? Why?

6. What does he believe is the most important aspect of childhood, home life and growing up?

7. What role did God play in his home, and his personal, religious, and general upbringing?

8. Did he have a large or small family? Did he enjoy having siblings? Why, or why not?

9. Did he have enough money, clothing and basic necessities growing up? What does money mean to him?

10. How was his relationship with his mother, father, relatives then? And now?

11. What were some of his dreams and hopes? How did he see himself in his youth? And now?

12. What are his educational background and job experiences? What were his goals and ambitions as a teenager? And now?

13. What does he believe are his natural talents and best gifts?

14. If he could change one thing about himself now, what would that be? Why? What would he replace it with? Why?

15. What does he believe are his strengths and weaknesses?

16. What is his favorite color, book, holiday, TV program, music, pastime, and discussion?

17. What are his views on family, community, church and life in general?

18. Who was his first real girlfriend? How did it end, and why?

19. What did he like or dislike about his past relationships? Does he still have strong feelings for anyone in the past?

20. Does he believe that each person has an ideal soul mate? How does he define the ideal woman?

21. If he had all the money in the world he wanted right now, what would he do with it?

22. If he could do or be anything he wanted, what would that be?

23. Who are his friends and the most important people in his life?

24. Is there anyone that he strongly dislikes? Who and why?

25. Does he have any prejudices (racism, sexism, religious discrimination, etc.)?

26. What is his political outlook?

27. Does he like where he lives now? Where would he like to eventually live (country, island, state, city, suburb, house, apartment, penthouse, ranch, etc.)?

28. Has he ever had any children from a past relationship? If yes, what is the current father-child relationship? Does he want to have children in the future? What type of father would he like to be (would he be strict, spoil them with too much pocket money, have long talks with them about life and God, etc.)?

29. What makes him happy, comfortable, and confident?

30. What are his views about God, Jesus, the Holy Spirit, life on earth and an afterlife in heaven?

These thirty questions are only a sampling of interesting and important discussion points that will help you to see deeply into his heart. Don't use them in particular order nor ask them as if you're administering an institutional exam. And by all means, do not photocopy them and ask him to complete the questionnaire list. Let them flow naturally throughout your conversations together. It's your relationship, so you should decide what feels comfortable to you. Pray and ask the Holy Spirit to help you add in many more and delete any which feel unnatural to you. This is a basic guideline to help him open up to you. Let him do most of the talking. If he is a natural talker, you may not have any need for the sample questions – just enjoy the conversation.

He will talk his way in love with you without any hidden or planned agenda. He will realize:

"I enjoy spending time with *this special woman.* I've told *her* secrets and things that I've never shared with anyone before. She's different – there's something about *her* that's unique and special. I've never met anyone like *her* before. I can be myself with *her* and I love having *her* in my life. She doesn't judge me negatively; she always looks out for my best and gives me *her* positive and kind suggestions.

I feel I can trust *her* enough to open myself to her. She is beautiful. I love *her* warmth and I love the way I feel when I'm around *her*. I look forward to spending time with *her*. I love being with *her*. In fact, I love *her*. I could see myself spending the rest of my life with *her*. In fact, I want *her* for my wife. *One day* I'm going to propose to *her*..."

The *her* he will be referring to is *you*. So, how do *you* "help" him, in a spiritually-sound manner, to propose *one day soon* (within six months), and not *one day somewhere down the road* (years from now)?

You are almost there, keep reading and let the Holy Spirit open your awareness, nourish your heart, and reveal God's truth of how your two human temples (mind, body and spirit) can become one sacred, ever-lasting, matrimonial bond...*soon!*

Spiritual Truth # 7:
"And Two Will Become One"

GETTING TO THE GOD-CENTERED "I DO"

It's really amazing what happens when you go behind the veil and enter into deep, purposeful, Holy Spirit-filled, *sanctified prayer*. When God's anointing and spiritual blessing is radiating from you, it sends out a magnetic force field and will attract many. But, you must try each spirit, to recognize your one true *sacred* match that you'll be stepping into "togetherness"and "forever" with.

Of all the testimonials I could share in this chapter, I want to have a heart-to-heart with you and pull back the curtain on my own sacred love and marriage because I've experienced this first hand and have walked-the-walk, and not just listened-to-the talk, on how to find your own true soul mate. I will set aside my professional psychological hat and ministerial garment, and simply sit and chat with you, woman-to-woman, sister-to-sister, friend-to-friend, in an open and honest spiritually-filled conversation that will turn things around in your favor. I promise you, this really works.

When you are venturing into deep *sanctified prayer* to ask God for your specific soul match, it is such a powerful and endearing experience that it can form an instant connection between two people. If you are not serious about removing the layers of preconceived notions and getting connected with your particular soul mate, then do not use the *sanctified prayer* until you've made up your mind and are really ready to walk in sacred love and matrimonial bliss with him.

Take a moment to think deeply about this Biblical truth: Instead of seeing yourself as a human being with a spirit, start to look at yourself as a spiritual being from God, having a human experience at this time on Earth. *You* were definitely a spirit before your body temple was formed in your mother's womb. In Jeremiah 1:4, God said, "Before I formed you in the belly I knew thee; and before you came out of the womb, I *sanctified* thee."

If you can believe this, then think outside of the box like I did, and realize that the same manner in which God has formed you and knows you, He also *has already* formed and knows the perfect match for you. What you have to do is learn how to enter into the Holy of Holies and pray for the Holy Spirit to arrange the opportunities for you to meet and recognize each other at some point [soon] during your journey on Earth.

Jesus shared this awesome truth in Matthew 19:5, 6 "For this cause a man shall leave father and mother and cleave [bond] to his wife and the twain shall be one flesh...What therefore God had joined together, let not man put asunder."

It wasn't until I *understood* the wisdom of this revelation that I was guided to have a soul-stirring, heart-to-heart, *sanctified prayer* with God to meet and recognize my very own sacred soul mate.

God answered my prayer.

I'm sure you're familiar with the popular saying "Be careful what you ask for, you may just get it." Based on experience I encourage you to alter it to "Be purposeful when you ask, for you will just get it." It's important to be purposeful because once you go into your prayer closet and really "ask" for a husband, you will be getting many admirers popping into your life "out of the blue." However, you must know what your purpose is in order to choose the one that's right for you, in a manner that's pleasing to God.

When I prayed to God for *a husband,* I received three proposals within one year. I was neither dating, nor courting any one. As a matter of fact, I was a "born-again virgin," deeply embedded in my career. Over the years, I had helped thousands of women and men to transform their unhealthy relationship track record and get into wholesome, happy, healthy, and compatible love relationships. I was busy writing book after book, traveling around the globe doing my signature relationship programs that were helping peoples lives, winning awards, and topping numerous bestseller list (all by the grace of God).

I was happily consumed with my work, because I was living on a purposeful career path. About five years ago, I took a break from my "busy" schedule, to take a breather and do a personal life evaluation. Here I was helping people by the thousands to form and have loving relationships, and there I was too busy to take the time do the same for myself. Just like you at this moment, I wanted to be in love and married. I was ready to fall in love. So,

I started to pray for *a husband.*

Forget the false notion and myth that you can't find love when looking for it. The key is to know where to look. I believed completely in the Biblical verse "seek and you shall find," so I went directly to the Creative Director of the Good Book – I went to God. I got more than I asked for (talk about an overflow!). I received *three* proposals all because I asked God with deep conviction. On the surface, they were all wonderful potential suitors, but all I needed was *one* – the *right one for me.* The first proposal was from a very handsome, kind, and intelligent psychotherapist, platonic friend and colleague of mine, who I had known for approximately eight years. We were simply friends, and after my deep prayer to God, he suddenly popped the question out of the blue, and he was quite serious. I was flattered and deeply moved, but I "looked before I leaped."

One of my close girlfriends remarked, "He's a good catch; he's gorgeous, charming, and financially-secure. I wouldn't let him get away!" I agree that he would probably make a terrific husband, but I wasn't sure if we belonged together because I wasn't feeling an inner conviction in my spirit. So, I prayed about it and politely turned down his proposal. The second one was from my college fiancé who I had not seen in fifteen years. (Talk about popping up out of the blue – it's amazing how prayer works.) I felt we were way too young to be engaged so many years ago, had broken our engagement over a decade and a half ago; he had since been married and divorced, and was currently in private practice as a successful anesthesiologist. And again, when he popped the question, I prayed and politely declined.

After this, I had a soul-stirring, heart-to-heart *sanctified prayer* with God, and instead of asking for *a husband,* I finally realized that I had to specifically ask Him for *my husband.*

Enter Richard. Here's the amazing thing, I had already briefly met Richard two years before and did not recognize at the time that one day our souls would open up, connect, and we'd be bonded in "togetherness forever." I couldn't see it, because I wasn't purposefully looking for a sacred soul mate at the time. When you hear this, doesn't it make you wonder if you've already met your sacred soul match, and have not recognized him yet? (You will after this.)

The Holy Spirit has a remarkable sense of humor. It makes me smile when I reflect on all that has transpired from the time of our first meeting, and wonder "What if I had recognized him from that moment?" According to him, he "knew" I was the one for him from day one.

We first met when Richard visited New York in July of 1999. He was a research scientist, geologist and a successful business owner in Jamaica, West Indies. He had come to visit his ailing dad. I knew his brother and sister-in-law and one day they all stopped by my home to say hello (I joke about it now, that my soul mate literally walked right up to my front door). When I first saw Richard, I thought he was handsome, intelligent, and very nice, but never even remotely entertained the thought of a relationship at the time, simply because I wasn't looking for it. We all went out on a sight-seeing tour and Richard and I enjoyed talking with each other. We had planned to see a couple more tourist attractions while he was in New York, but unfortunately his five-week trip was cut short due to his father's death.

I had no inkling that he was attracted to me at all, but when he left, I somehow wished we had gotten to know each other better. Anyhow, I quickly blocked out that feeling as I threw myself back into my work. During the two year span before we reconnected, I had given many seminars and workshops on the island of Jamaica. Richard was doing research at the University of the West Indies, and was either teaching chemistry or lecturing on some other neighboring island each time I was there, so we never saw each other.

Actually, we had no direct contact until I had my *sanctified prayer* with God. During this time, I was under contract as the "on-air, after-care and staff psychologist" for the *Queen Latifah* TV talk show, and also enrolled in seminary, studying Urban Ministry, full-time. I had two very good classmates and platonic-friends who became my protective older brothers; one was an assistant pastor, and the other was a pastor-in-training; both would always cover me in prayer. It was a few weeks before Christmas when I opened my soul up to Heaven and prayed my own personal *sanctified prayer* to God.

Have you ever had one of those belly-jerking, heart-wrenching, soul-searching, tear-staining prayers, where you pray until you just can't pray any more? Well, it was one of those. I am not going to gloss it over for you, and pretend it was a dainty little prayer that just rolled off the tip of my tongue. I was tearfully on the floor, in front of my Creator, petitioning, and being Comforted by the Holy Spirit, for what seemed like hours. I wasn't just praying for a husband, I wanted "my" husband.

Anyone can have a husband, but when you really want *your* husband, be prepared to go the extra mile – go to God completely vulnerable and naked without being clothed with false pride, a shallow emotional shopping list, and a barrier around your soul. Believe me, God already knows who you are and what you need. He wants you to come to Him first and he will bless you wholeheartedly. You can read this spiritual truth for yourself in Matthew 6:32-33, "Your heavenly Father knows that ye have need for all these things. But seek ye first the kingdom of God, and his righteousness, and all these things shall be given to you." Trust me on this – many people have spouses, but look at the divorce and infidelity statistics – this is because they have not bonded with the right soul match, so disrespect, cheating, abuse, and estrangement slip into their relationships. With your sacred match, you don't ever have to worry about any of this because at the pinnacle of your God-centered union will be trust, joy, understanding, respect and *pure* love.

My prayer was purposeful because I had to make sure that I had stayed on God's path and not been affected by any old family patterns (or "generational curses" in the spiritual realm). I had to choose wisely. Those of you who are reading this and familiar with my previous books will know that both my natural mother and aunt made bad relationship choices that ultimately robbed them of their lives exactly twenty years apart. They were both murdered by the hands of their ill-matched suitors. When I was 10 years old, I witnessed my mother being shot to death, six bullets in her head by her obsessive ex-lover who became a stalker. Then twenty years later, her older sister was stabbed forty times and butchered by her common-law, possessive husband. Aunt Gloria's killer used to be in church every Sunday, but "church" was never in him. He was just sitting in the pews, taking up space, without the true spirit of God operating in him. All this to say, don't let anyone's outward appearance fool you. Try his spirit; use each step in this entire book and take it "all" to the Lord in prayer.

I thank God for a grandmother who taught me how to pray from as early as I can remember. If it wasn't for a personal prayer life and a direct connection with God, I probably wouldn't be alive to share this testimony and message of hope with you from these pages. I probably would have repeated the dysfunctional pattern that unfortunately and unknowingly was set in motion by the horrible experiences that happened to my mother and aunt.

But at a very young age, I was blessed with spiritual wisdom way beyond my years. I made a promise to myself and to God that I would never follow the unhealthy path. I learned how to break the cycle before the cycle broke me. I refused to ever become a negative love statistic in life.

I want to encourage you to realize that you are not responsible for where you came from, but you are responsible for where you're going, and for how you choose from this moment on. Learn from the past, but don't dwell in the past. Don't ever belittle, doubt and think less of yourself because of any unhealthy family tree, or past unhealthy relationship choice.

My prayer for you at this moment is that God blesses you with a healthy, secure, God-respecting, kind man who is going to love, cherish, adore, and respect you without ever lifting a finger to hurt you, raising a voice to belittle you, or ruining your trust by lying to you. You deserve to have the best; don't settle for less than ideal. Use Holy Spirit-filled prayer and openly ask God to help you, mold you in His image, lift you to a higher spiritual level, and attract the man who's equally-yoked. The one who He has already made just for you.

It doesn't matter what you have or haven't done in the past. You may have made some mistakes, but you are not a mistake. "If anyone be in Christ, she is a new creation, old things have passed away, behold, all things have become new." (2 Corinthians 5:17)

While you were reading each chapter in this book, God was creating something new at each stage within you. Isn't this awesome? He has been preparing you to encounter your hand-picked groom, just like the parable about the ten virgins in The New Testament's Matthew 25: 1-13. The five wise ones were prepared by keeping oil in their lamps to give them light (they kept hopeful), while the five foolish ones gave up hope that if the groom hadn't come into their life as yet, he probably never would. Unfortunately, they lost their focus, lost their hope, lost their oil, therefore, their lights went out.

Jesus encourages in Matthew 5:16 that you

"Let your light shine so bright before men, that they may see [recognize] your good works [your substance], and glorify [give thanks for you] your Father which is in heaven." The unbelieving women probably laughed at the hopeful, prepared women, saying, "Why bother, it's a myth; he probably won't come; maybe he's already taken, so why waste time preparing for something that may never happen?"

Don't react to the negative attack

Don't *you* ever give up hope, or let anyone talk you out of being prepared for your sacred soul mate. Because when the *sacred groom* did appear, at God's appointed time, the five wise women that keep their lights and hopes shining could clearly "recognize" him, while the others who gave up hope couldn't see the truth standing in front of them. They couldn't see anything because their lamps went out, all because of lack of preparation and disbelief. When they finally realized that the sacred groom was real and available to all who believe, they scurried around at the last minute, trying to partake in some of the blessings of the prepared women. They wanted what the wise women had – they begged for some of their oil.

When your soul match stands in front of you, don't you let anyone try to hold you back, trip you on your track, or mess up your appointed time with destiny by their interference, criticism, and delinquency. The five unprepared ones tried to stall the five wise women from going out to meet their sacred groom. They came running up to them saying,

"We are not prepared; we have no oil in our lamps; our lights have gone out, so we cannot see our way to him – please share with us what you have." The five who had always kept hopeful (and prayerful) were wise enough to not let interference cause them to stumble, be sidetracked, or lose their focus. They said, "If we stop to give you some of what we have, we won't have enough to keep our own lights shining at this, and to see our way on the path to him."

The wise, prepared women became sacred brides to their very own sacred groom, while the unprepared ones were left, trying to get prepared at the last minute. They missed out on all the blessings and matrimonial bliss because they didn't believe the *sanctified truth;* they didn't believe that the *sacred bond* would really happen.

> **Therefore shall a man leave his father and his mother, and shall cleave [bond] unto his wife, and they shall be one flesh.**
> (Genesis 2:24)

Don't you miss out. Be one of the hopeful, wise, prepared women. Make sure you stretch your belief toward a loving Creator who always provides what He promises. Where God guides, he provides. I believed and I encourage you to do the same. I prayed a *sanctified prayer* to my Maker with heart wide-open and spirit *completely* surrendered to Him. And, a little over a month, approximately forty days (I'm not kidding), by mid-January, Richard's brother, "out of the blue," finally confessed, "My brother has been in love with you from the first day he laid eyes on you. We speak on the phone each week and for the past two years the first thing that comes out of his mouth *every* time is, 'How is Grace; have you heard from her; is she okay; I'd like to have her number; is she back in New York yet?' I haven't given him your new number and I've never told you how he feels because you're a busy career woman who is always traveling. I just assumed you wouldn't have time for a relationship."

Has something similar ever happened to you? Take note: Sometimes even when your closest blood relative or friend assume that they are doing something noble by deciding what's best for you, without your permission, they could be erroneously interfering with or stalling your destiny, no matter how innocent or well-meaning they may be. However, when the prayers go up, the blessings come down. Keep praying because *"Whatsoever is truly yours, can never be taken away from you,"* even after years have passed with no direct contact.

Delayed but not denied

Please keep this in mind – your soul match may be delayed by a series of circumstances, or outside interference, or because your conviction has not been strong enough at this point, but once you open up to the Creator with *sanctified prayer*, you will not be denied.

It was a Saturday afternoon when Richard's brother made his confession, after two years of deliberately keeping silent (by the way, Richard and I laugh about this now); but he still did not volunteer the number at that point. However, I did a quick, silent prayer and consulted: "God, you know my heart and what I've been praying for. If this could be it, then clear the barrier and provide a clear pathway in Jesus' name. Amen." That was it.

His brother, without any clue, just reached for the phone in the living room, dialed a number, handed me the receiver, and walked into the kitchen to talk with my sister and sister-in-law.

When Richard and I spoke and reconnected after not being in touch in two years, I immediately felt a feeling of "deep comfort." We both were surprised and so excited to "finally" speak to each other that we were practically lost for words and didn't know what to say – we couldn't speak (isn't this funny – wait until it happens to you – make sure you write and tell me all about it). I managed to quickly reel off my phone number to him, before hanging up from our brief ten-minute call. Then, I started to wonder if he understood the number at the marathon pace at which I relayed it. I then realized that in our excitement, I forgot to write down his number.

You must know when to put your feelings on hold, and know when to be bold. I went to join the others who had now moved into the dining area, and my comment to his brother was, "What's his number?"

Fast forward to four days later: Richard hadn't called. It's a good thing I had been bold enough to ask for his number, I prayed about it, braced myself, and used it that Wednesday evening. Sometimes when a car has been parked in a garage for too long you have to give it a gentle, little jump start. He was so happy to hear from me, all I said was a kind and friendly, "Hello." (Remember in Chapter Four I shared with you that most men are afraid of rejection, even the most courageous, successful, wealthy, handsome and God-fearing ones, and all you have to do is be polite with a warm and friendly non-threatening "hello" to initiate a conversation.)

After my initial "hello" jump-started him into my life, I never had to initiate another phone call again (we laugh about it all the time now). Richard called me every morning, noon, and/or evening. The sun never went down on any given day without us talking with each other. Just wait until you and your ideal match recognize each other – the little, romantic sweet-nothings will play a big part in your relationship. We had a long-distance telephone courtship for the first three months. We talked about everything under the sun. I would start a sentence, and he would finish; he would start, and I would finish. We shared so much in common that it was almost surreal. But I've learned to not question, but to accept and give God thanks for my blessings even if by worldly definition, they may seem "too good to be true." That's when you thank God even more and seal the deal on a spiritual level with Him first.

I felt he was "the one." He felt the same about me, and within a short period we had talked and prayed our way in love with each other. But to put our deep courtship to the ultimate test, three months later, I prayed another *sanctified prayer* and asked the Holy Spirit to reveal the truth to me. My prayer consisted of three definite things:

1. God, if this is the right man for me, above all let him love You first and foremost.

2. Next, let him have had a genuinely good upbringing with no emotional baggage and really *like* who he is (with a healthy sense of self).

3. Finally, let him be able to love me as much as he loves himself.

No one but God knew this personal request of mine. I placed it on the altar of my heart and believed the Holy Spirit would show me the truth. As surely as I share the following details with you, I am positive that if you really believe, you will definitely receive and recognize your own sacred love when you are ready and release it to God. It is so real!

Guess what – approximately two weeks after petitioning God with my prayer, I was lying on my couch, talking with Richard on the phone when, "out of the blue," he confessed, "Grace, I have to share something with you. I couldn't feel this way about you if you weren't so spiritually connected to God because God is the guiding force in my life, and *I love Him more than anything or anyone.* I didn't come from a rich family, but all my basic needs were met. I grew up with a lot of love and excellent education. When I look back at my upbringing, I have no regrets and I wouldn't change any thing. *I had a good childhood – I really like my life and I love who I am.* And, with the very breath in my body, *I love you just as much."*

Plop! I fell off my couch! I hit the floor as

reality hit me. At that exact moment in time, I *knew* he was "the one." (Thank you, God!) Finally, I'd recognized the wonderful soul whom I'd be sharing and spending the rest of my life with. I waited patiently, prayed purposely, and believed whole-heartedly – *and God answered.*

This is the very same God who is answering you right now – believe it:

> **All things for which you pray and ask, *believe***
> **that you have received them,**
> **and you shall have them.**
> (Mark 11:24)

A couple of months following my sacred revelation, a popular TV talk show host and friend of mine called me at home to ask, "How do you know if he's the one?"

"Girl, all I can tell you is, I honestly have never felt this love for anyone before and have him love me so much at the same time. The best way I can describe it is, it feels as if God is in heaven, holding a sacred golden cord in the palm of His hands, and one end of the string is fastened to Richard's bellybutton, and the other is attached to mine. It seems as if we are kindred spirits, reflecting the two halves of each other's soul. And on top of that, we make sure to pray for each other."

"Wow! That's amazing," she exclaimed. "That soul mate stuff really works! It should be part of your wedding vows."

It was! Richard and I were married a few months later.

The couple that *prays* together, *stays* together.

> **Sanctify them through the truth. And for their sakes, I sanctify myself, that they also might be sanctified through the truth. That they may be one, as thou Father, art one in me, and I in thee, that they may also be one in us.**
> (St. John 17: 17 & 21)

7 Essential Sacred Bonding Tips:

1. Share similar spiritual beliefs, interests and values.

2. Talk things out.

3. Be honest, sincere, and compassionate.

4. Be your true self, but be each other's best friend.

5. Set some private time aside to pamper and take care of yourself.

6. Learn to laugh together.

7. Practice the *three prayers*:

-*pray* by yourself
-*pray* with each other
-*pray* for each other

---

1. My special prayer *for him* is:

_____

_____

_____

_____

_____

2. My special prayer *for me* is:

_____

_____

_____

_____

_____

3. My special prayer *for us* is:

_____

_____

_____

_____

_____

Here's the *sanctified prayer* I used for my supernatural hookup from God. Feel free to use it as your own, but by all means incorporate your own words as the Holy Spirit moves you:

> **Dear God, I know You didn't put me on the earth to be alone. I really want the right husband for me. It is Your words that say 'it is not good for me to be alone, and two shall bond together and become one.' Father, if unconditional love really exists, then please let me experience it before I complete my journey on Earth. Please let me know what it's like to love someone wholeheartedly without any fear; and let him love me unconditionally at the same time.**
>
> **God, I know that You are the Alpha and the Omega, the beginning and the end, the Creator of all the universe, and without You nothing is made. That's why I come to You now, as Your daughter, asking You to let me experience real love. Not a needy or unhealthy love, but a sacred Holy Spirit-filled love with You at the center. God, use me as an example that others can see that true love still exists the way You originally created it to be. Bond us together in holy matrimony that we may reflect a pure, clean, and enjoyable love.**
>
> **Father God, in the name of Jesus, I ask that You hand-pick my special husband for me now. I know that You've already made him, and I pray that the Holy Spirit brings us together in one accord. Lord, I am thanking You in advance, because I believe Jesus when He said, "Whatever I ask for in His name, believing, then I will have it."**
>
> **God, I believe; I now receive and I thank You. I love You; I respect You; I worship You. Thank You.**

(Amen!)

There you have it! Go ahead and ask, believe, and receive your very own divine, sacred connection...

...Oh, by the way, please send me a wedding invitation (smiles)!

About The Author

Spiritual psychologist Dr. Grace Cornish is the winner of the 2004 "Woman of The Year" Award from the prestigious Woman of Substance Ministries, Inc.

Dr. Grace is the bestselling author of nine enormously popular books, a nationally-recognized keynote speaker of sold-out seminars, a minister of The Word, and one of the country's foremost relationship consultants.

After overcoming the early childhood tragedy of seeing her mother brutally murdered in front of her, Dr. Grace became determined that her life's mission would be helping women and men in unhealthy relationships to overcome all forms of abuse, build self-worth, and find equal balance of respect and healthy love.

Dr. Grace, who has a Ph.D. in Social Psychology and a Masters (MPS) in Urban Ministry, is renowned for her award-winning training programs, *Rewriting Your Life's Script* and *Turning Stumbling Blocks Into Stepping Stones*. The format of her groundbreaking program *Face It, Erase It and Replace It*, is being used as a guideline by many counselors, pastors and therapists across the country.

She is known to millions of television viewers from her regular appearances on many diverse shows, including *Good Day New York, John Walsh, Ricki Lake,* and *Conversations With Ed Gordon.* For two years, she served as the on-air and after-care staff psychologist for the *Queen Latifah* show.

Dr. Grace's trademark brand of charismatic, compassionate, and smart counseling has yielded her repeat appearances on a wide variety of programs on *NBC, CBS, FOX-TV, WOR-TV, PAX-TV,* and *BET-TV.* She is frequently featured, interviewed, and quoted in such magazines as *Essence, Ebony, Jet, Heart & Soul* and *Upscale.*

Dr. Grace has received a number of honors, including recognition by *Who's Who in America, Who's Who in The East,* and *Who's Who in Writers, Editors & Poets.* She is happily married and lives with her husband and daughter in Westchester County, New York.

ALSO BY DR. GRACE CORNISH

The Band-Aid Bond

You Deserve Healthy Love, Sis!

*10 Good Choices That Empower
Black Women's Lives*

10 Bad Choices That Ruin Black Women's Lives

Radiant Women of Color

Radiant Woman of Color (Compact Edition)

Think And Grow Beautiful

The Fortune of Being Yourself

La Fortuna De Ser Una Misma

**FORTHCOMING FROM DR. GRACE
CORNISH-LIVINGSTONE**

The Matrimonial Bond
♡♡
What To Do After The "I Do"

For publication date contact:
e-mail: drgcornish@aol.com
or visit: www.drcornish.com

Praises for Dr. Grace's life-enhancing and relationship programs...

"Dr. Grace shows you how you can finally have the healthy, rich, spiritually nurturing relationship you desire and deserve! Let's face it, no one understands the unique relationship issues plaguing women like she does. Now she's back with her trademark "tell it like it is" approach to teach you how to achieve long-lasting love—it's the remedy you've been searching for!"
                                                            —*Doubleday Direct*

"We keep inviting Dr. Grace back because she's simply the best!!!"
                                                            —*Good Day New York*

"Back by popular demand! Dr. Grace is an empowering speaker you won't want to miss."   —*Barnes & Noble*

"An author who clearly understands her audience Cornish provides warm explanations that are personal yet universal, and steers women towards better lives with a firm and loving hand."
                                                            —*Publishers Weekly*

"She was amazing! We had more walk-ins for Dr. Grace than for any of our other speakers. While she was in town, she appeared on two local TV news programs—our *NBC* and *FOX* affiliates. Many of our walk-ins saw her on either of those shows and just had to come to the program. This was the largest group yet—we even had to have more chairs brought in! One group traveled 60 miles just to see her. Dr. Grace is such a nice woman—so generous with her time, talent and spirit!"
                                                            —*Covenant Healthcare,*
                                                            Women's Well-Being ™ Series

"When the Doctor is in, she draws a crowd!"
                                                            —*The Atlanta Daily*

For more information about Dr. Grace, contact:
Dr. Grace Cornish,
c/o MCDONALD-LIVINGSTONE,
786 Bronx River Road, Suite B-33
Bronxville, New York, 10708
Web:www.drcornish.com or call 212-576-8811